TRANSFORMING CONFLICT IN YOUR CHURCH:

A Practical Guide

Marlin E. Thomas
Editor

Herald
Press

Scottdale, Pennsylvania
Waterloo, Ontario

Library of Congress Cataloging-in-Publication Data

Transforming conflict in your church : a practical guide / Marlin Thomas, editor.
   p. cm.
Includes bibliographical references.
ISBN 0-8361-9197-8 (pbk. : alk. paper)
1. Conflict management—Religious aspects—Christianity. 2. Conflict management—Religious
   aspects—Mennonites. I. Thomas, Marlin E.
BV4597.53.C58 T73 2002
250—dc21

2001006881

TRANSFORMING CONFLICT IN YOUR CHURCH
Copyright © 2002 by Herald Press, Scottdale, Pa. 15683
   Published simultaneously in Canada by Herald Press,
   Waterloo, Ont. N2L 6H7. All rights reserved
Library of Congress Catalog Card Number: 2001006881
International Standard Book Number: 0-8361-9197-8
Printed in the United States of America
Book and cover design by Jim Butti
Cartoons by Joel Kauffmann (cover, 28, 41, 43, 48)

10 09 08 07 06 05 04   10 9 8 7 6 5 4 3

To order or request information, please call
1-800-759-4447 (individuals); 1-800-245-7879 (trade).
Website: www.mph.org

Table of Contents

Foreword

Congregations usually regard conflict as trouble to be avoided. Conflicts can lead to destructive behavior and structures in congregations, diminishing the work of the church. But conflict is also inevitable and can be understood as a normal part of personal and congregational life. Seen in this way, conflict can be a part of a healthy transformation process, strengthening congregations in their ministries.

Congregations that have experienced conflict and those who minister to them in the midst of conflict have been seeking tools to help interpret the health of congregations and to bring about positive changes and growth when struggles arise. *Transforming Conflict in Your Church: A Practical Guide* provides assessment tools that meet this need. The resources in this manual provide a useful means of measuring the health of congregations and a road map for addressing the causes of conflict in positive ways. The manual addresses various areas that are important in understanding congregational life and conflict, including communication, leadership, and decision making.

Congregations, pastors, and those who work with congregations will find this guide to be invaluable in seeking to prevent conflict and in working toward harmony when conflict arises. The tools provided will assist congregations not only in assessing conflict, but also in knowing when outside consultants and resources are needed. The manual can also assist leadership teams in understanding each other and their views of conflict, and how they as leaders respond both personally and corporately to conflict.

This guide emerges from the vision of the editor, Marlin Thomas, and from his conversations with church leaders. The tools in this manual have been tested in congregations and shaped by the experiences of congregational consultants. The manual has already proven to be helpful to pastors as well as congregational leaders and consultants. Congregations can experience transformation as they develop clarity of vision that will assist them in their mission as a community of faith.

Healthy congregations tend to be evangelistic and invite others into the fellowship of believers. This manual will assist in that essential ministry. Overseers, conference ministers, pastors, and congregational members will find that this manual provides resources to do the work of Christ more effectively in the twenty-first century.

—Dale Stoltzfus
Codirector of the Office of Ministerial Leadership, Mennonite Church USA
Overseer, Lancaster Conference

Editor's Preface

Everyone who works with churches, and everyone who works in a church, knows that conflict exists—*even in churches*. Sometimes conflict strengthens churches, but all too often it weakens the church and its ministries. Everyone wishes for a magic cure so the work of ministry may go forward, but no such magic cure exists.

Conflict even abounds in the pages of Scripture—within people, between people, within groups, and between groups. Sometimes it was handled in a godly fashion, and other times it was not. When it was, the participants in the conflict grew spiritually and went on to serve God better. It is the desire of the authors of this manual that God's people today may be led to discover better ways to resolve their conflicts, so they, too, may grow spiritually and serve God in uninhibited ways.

This manual is the direct outgrowth of several conversations between church leaders and the editor, about ways to put a tool into the hands of congregational leaders that would assist them in addressing internal conflict before it got out of hand, as well as guide them in determining when and how to seek outside assistance.

A word of caution: This manual is most culturally appropriate for those who trace their cultural heritage to northern Europe. It assumes that organizational health includes open, direct communication. For many of the world's cultures indirect communication is preferred, particularly where there is potential for conflict. Context matters in conflict, and we recommend that those who are not part of this manual's primary audience obtain the assistance of an experienced cross-cultural interpreter for assistance in using it.

The Congregational Conflict Type Indicator (CCTI), with which this manual begins, is a thirty-two question assessment tool designed to provide insights into five different arenas of conflict that are frequently found in churches. They are the arenas of Boundaries, Communication, Decision making, Interpersonal Relationships, and Leadership. It is suggested that members of congregational leadership teams secure their own personal copy of this manual, and complete the CCTI before reading through the manual. It is then also suggested that the leadership team develop a plan by which they can work through the manual together, discussing insights and learning together as they go. If needed, an outside process person or consultant may be secured to assist in this process. After purchase of enough copies of the manual for the entire leadership team, additional copies of the CCTI may be accessed via the Mennonite Publishing House website (www.mph.org/books/transformingconflict.htm) for wider use in the congregation, if desired.

Chapter 1 provides a brief, basic description about how conflict works, for those who find themselves involved in conflict without understanding what's happening to them and their church. Chapter 2 then describes the five levels of conflict a congregation might experience, and what to do about conflict at each level. Chapter 3 discusses some ways in which the church "system" can fail, allowing conflict to get out of hand, and provides some insights into dealing with those system failures. Chapter 4 provides insights into what congregations can do to work through low-level conflicts themselves. Chapter 5 provides assistance in understanding how to seek outside assistance in working through more intense conflict.

The appendices provide additional resources for those who may need them. The "Levels of Conflict Evaluator" in Appendix A provides another way to understand the type and intensity of the conflict the congregation may be experiencing. Appendix B provides a list of several Conflict Management Styles Instruments for those who may want to take that approach to understanding how to manage conflict. Appendixes C and D provide an extensive bibliography of resources in conflict transformation, as well as a list of resourcing networks and agencies in the United States and Canada. Appendix E provides additional background information for one of the work projects suggested in chapter 1.

Several Mennonite mediators provided valuable insights and effort in helping to complete this project. Richard Blackburn, Larry Dunn, Alice Price, Duane Ruth-Heffelbower, Carolyn Schrock-Shenk, and I spent an intense, tightly packed day putting together the skeletal framework for this manual, and developing the questions for the Congregational Conflict Type Indicator. They were generously hosted by members of Beth-El Mennonite Church, Colorado Springs, Colorado. Larry, Alice, Duane, and I each contributed to the writing of the manual, and I provided the general editorial guidance that brought this project to completion. Ron Zabel, of Conflict Resolution and Conciliation Services, Fairfax, Virginia, provided additional editorial reading and advice. We express our deep gratitude and appreciation to all for their generous contribution to this project.

Mennonite congregational leaders across the United States and Canada assisted in field testing this manual, to help the authors and editor make it as readable and usable for the average pastor and lay leader as possible. These congregations came from the wide spectrum of Mennonites, including several Mennonite Brethren congregations, and included small and large congregations as well as urban and rural communities, scattered from the Pacific coast to the Atlantic coast, and from the South to the North (including Canada). Several conference ministers and denominational leaders also provided their reflections and suggestions. Statistical and technical data relating to the field testing of this manual may be secured by e-mailing marlin.thomas@rrcinc.org.

This project could not have been accomplished without a generous grant from The Showalter Foundation of Newton, Kansas, with additional assistance from Mennonite Conciliation Service, Akron, Pennsylvania. We are deeply indebted to them, as well as to all those who helped us in so many ways to make this project possible. May it be a useful tool in the hands of God to untie the cords of conflict in many places, setting God's people free for the work of ministry to which they have been called.

—*Marlin E. Thomas*
  Lancaster, Pennsylvania

Congregational Conflict Type Indicator
(Form E)

(Permission is hereby granted to congregations who purchase copies of this manual for elders or board members, to make additional copies of this CCTI for congregational use only. The CCTI may also be accessed on the Mennonite Publishing House website at www.mph.org/books/transformingconflict.htm)

Introduction. This Congregational Conflict Type Indicator is based on the assumption that an appropriate whole-group, open process is the healthiest way to develop congregational life. Any group of responsible individuals in the congregation may participate in this congregational conflict type indicator. It is suggested that (at least) those people who are currently active in leadership agree to complete the instrument. Following completion of the instrument it is suggested that the group meet together to compile the scores and discuss the implications of the composite scores, as directed below. (Persons from cultures valuing top down leadership, and indirect communication in conflict resolution, may not find this tool helpful in the form presented here.)

Instructions. Each person should work alone. Circle only one response for each question. Think of your congregation as a whole. In cases where you feel more than one response is true, circle *only* the *one* that is generally true of most situations in your congregation, based upon your personal, firsthand knowledge. Do not spend time analyzing any question or discussing it with anyone else. Your honest, "first impression" answers to all questions can assist your leadership group in developing better and healthier approaches to congregational life when responding to conflict situations.

1. When people don't like a decision the congregation makes
   a. They denounce the decision at the time it is being made and refuse to accept it
   b. They participate actively in the decision-making process and accept it after it is made
   c. They do not object or complain about the decision, but do not cooperate after it is made

2. Information concerning congregational life is generally communicated through
   a. The congregational grapevine
   b. A variety of written and oral means
   c. Official documents only

3. When discussing important issues in church meetings, leaders
   a. Tend to be hesitant or unclear in sharing their views, so we're never sure where they stand
   b. Are clear in communicating where they stand while also inviting others to express their views
   c. Tend to share their views in authoritarian tones

4. In our church,
   a. I know of sexual violations by leaders or others, but we don't do anything about it except maybe talk to them
   b. I know of sexual violations by leaders or others that are being addressed according to biblical and denominational guidelines
   c. I know of sexual violations by leaders or others that no one wants to talk about
   d. I don't know of any sexual violations by leaders or others

5. When people in the congregation disagree
   a. They tell others their side of the story
   b. They talk to the one they disagree with
   c. They avoid everyone in church

6. When defining congregational direction and purpose, leaders
   a. Either hold back or lack the ability to articulate vision, leaving it entirely to the congregation
   b. Articulate their own vision, while working with others in the congregation to clarify a common vision
   c. Tend to pursue their own vision without inviting input from the congregation

7. In our church the real decisions are made by
   a. The "pillars" of the church
   b. The appropriate board or committee of the church
   c. The pastor

8. When people in our congregation discuss a situation
   a. They argue and try to get their own way
   b. They speak to each other in a way that leads to understanding
   c. They don't listen well to what others say

9. The amount of information about key church issues shared with the congregation is
   a. Overwhelming
   b. About right
   c. Inadequate

10. Most evaluation of church programs and staff performance occurs
    a. On the grapevine
    b. By an appropriate oversight team
    c. By strong personalities in the congregation, perhaps including the "founders" or the "inner circle" of the church

11. During times of crisis or tension in the congregation, leaders tend to
    a. Become reactive or too emotional
    b. Remain calm, and focus on listening to others
    c. Distance themselves from people who disagree with them

12. When someone fails in a church job, we
    a. Criticize them publicly
    b. Give them as much encouragement and support as we can
    c. Criticize them privately

13. Information sharing about important decisions most often happens
    a. Only when disagreements arise
    b. At each stage of the decision-making process
    c. Only after a decision has already been made

14. We conduct evaluations
    a. Only of the pastor
    b. Of all the congregational ministries
    c. Only when something goes wrong

15. Past conflicts or painful events in our congregational life
    a. Regularly creep into discussions and decisions about the present in the form of blaming, shaming, or judging
    b. Are referred to in discussions and decisions about the present so we can learn from them
    c. Are carefully avoided by everyone

16. People of different ethnic groups
    a. Are welcome in our church if they don't try to change us
    b. Enrich the church
    c. Need their own churches

17. Congregational meetings are generally used to
    a. Air grievances or contest leadership decisions
    b. Share information and allow discussion of different viewpoints
    c. Rubber-stamp the decisions of leadership

18. Different points of view over biblical interpretation
    a. Get people all stirred up
    b. Can lead to spiritual growth
    c. Are unacceptable in our church

19. When serious conflict breaks out in our congregation
    a. People just leave without giving us a chance to talk about the disagreement
    b. People choose to leave only after talking about the disagreements and agreeing that it is appropriate to leave
    c. Almost no one leaves, but no one changes his or her view either

20. When problems arise in the congregation
    a. No one seems to be willing to take any responsibility for the problem
    b. We tend to share responsibility for addressing the problem
    c. We tend to blame the pastor or others in the church

21. We have a variety of church activities
    a. Which are optional for everyone
    b. Which appeal to different people
    c. Which everyone is expected to attend

22. People with concerns about congregational life or leadership issues often feel
    a. Free to share these concerns however and whenever they wish
    b. Comfortable with designated channels for processing these concerns
    c. Confused about when, where, and whether to process these concerns

23. When a decision must be made
    a. We can't seem to bring closure to any decision, but keep shaping and reshaping it to fit everybody's wants
    b. We try to help people feel safe in expressing differing opinions and use their insights to help shape the proposal
    c. We move as quickly as possible, to avoid derailing it by discussion of different opinions

24. When I make decisions about something related to congregational life I
    a. State my position and don't budge
    b. Calmly explain my point of view but remain open to other people's ideas
    c. Don't commit myself until I know others agree with me

25. When a person or group in our congregation makes a decision, those who don't like it
    a. Form a group to overturn the decision
    b. Ask for clarification and offer their insights
    c. Refuse to talk to that person or group

26. In our congregation rules and bylaws
    a. Are only referred to in times of crisis
    b. Serve as a guide for our group life in helpful ways
    c. Enslave us at every turn

27. When a problem arises we tend to
    a. Generalize a lot about each other and our church
    b. Be clear and specific about the problems
    c. Hold back on information and remain vague

28. When conflicts occur between members of the leadership group
    a. Everyone finds out about it almost right away
    b. Appropriate guidelines for confidentiality and information-sharing are followed
    c. Almost no one ever finds out about it

29. If someone reveals information about congregational life or leadership activities that may be potentially damaging, that person will be
    a. Allowed to spread the information with no constraints
    b. Taken seriously and the information evaluated appropriately
    c. Cut off from fellowship by congregational members

30. When people or groups make decisions about church life or activities
    a. They are communicated so poorly they are misunderstood
    b. They are communicated clearly through written and oral announcements
    c. Very few people find out about it

31. When we have had serious conflict with others in the past, we
    a. Continue to find ways to hurt them and try to reform them if possible
    b. Address the hurts, give and receive forgiveness, and seek ways to build a stronger and better relationship
    c. Cut ourselves off from them and pretend they do not exist

32. When people or groups make decisions about congregational life
    a. They are criticized for being too dictatorial
    b. They are affirmed for their best efforts
    c. They only hear from those who don't like the decision

Individual Score Sheet

Scoring Instructions

Count the number of (a)s, (b)s, and (c)s circled. Place the total number for each group of scores on the line below in the correct section. If you are working by yourself, study this page and then go to page 15 for a more detailed analysis of your responses. If you are working with a group, transfer your numbers below to the Congregational Score Sheet.

(a) _____ (b) _____ (c) _____

Interpretation

The authors of this congregational conflict indicator are committed to developing healthy congregations based on a model of congregational interaction best described by (b) responses. If no more than 5% of your responses are located in section (a) or section (c), and at least ninety percent of your responses are located in section (b) your congregation may be viewed as an exceptionally healthy congregational system in the way it manages conflict. If as many as fifteen percent of your responses fall in either section (a) or (c) your congregation merits further study and evaluation. If fewer than sixty percent of your responses are located in section (b) your congregation may benefit from more in-depth assistance from an outside professional conflict consultant.

(a) responses point to a more erratic, hyperreactive response to disagreement. In general this means that members of the congregation overreact to difficult events in congregational life. Their emotions are loose and uncontrolled, and they have difficulty assessing the relative importance of different levels of distress. Further conversation or assistance would be helpful in learning how to respond to difficult situations in congregational life with less anxiety.

(b) responses point to a healthier, more balanced, whole-group process in response to disagreement. In general, this means that members of the congregation react appropriately to difficult events in congregational life. Their emotions are balanced and under control. They are able to respect one another and discern appropriate responses to a variety of conflict situations in congregational life.

(c) responses point to a more closed, underreactive response to disagreement. In general this means that members of the congregation underreact to difficult events in congregational life. Their emotions are tight and frozen, and joy is seldom expressed freely. Further conversation or assistance would be helpful in learning how to respond to difficult situations in congregational life with openness and integrity.

Congregational Score Sheet

Scoring Instructions

1. Transfer the (a), (b), and (c) scores from the individual score sheets of each person who completed this survey (above) into the grid on the next page. Place those numbers in the grid in the section corresponding to each score.

2. Add the scores in each box, and place the total number for each box in the first blank below the line.

3. Secure the total number of all responses by adding the composite scores of (a) + (b) + (c) = _____ .

4. Secure the percentage of (a), (b), and (c) responses by dividing each section score by the total number of scores. Place the percentages in the final set of blanks. The three percentage scores should equal 100 percent.

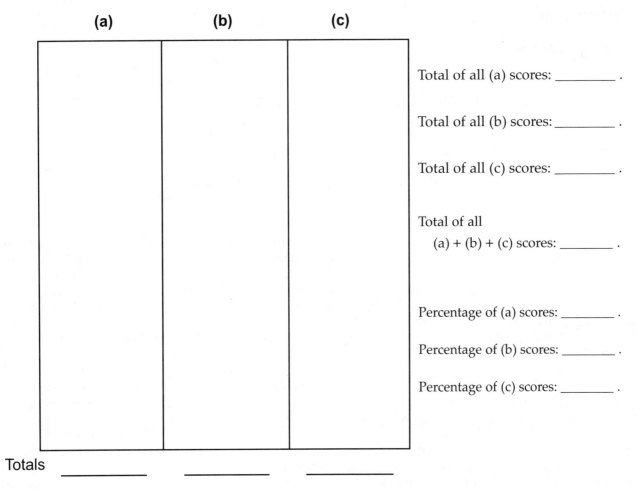

Total of all (a) scores: _____ .

Total of all (b) scores: _____ .

Total of all (c) scores: _____ .

Total of all
    (a) + (b) + (c) scores: _____ .

Percentage of (a) scores: _____ .

Percentage of (b) scores: _____ .

Percentage of (c) scores: _____ .

Totals _____ _____ _____

Interpretation

This Congregational Conflict Type Indicator seeks to identify five areas of congregational life in which destructive, unhealthy conflict can occur. They are Interpersonal relationships, Communication/ Information sharing, Decision making, Leadership, and Boundaries development. Identification of the questions which are included in each scale, or arena of conflict, may be secured by referring to "A More Detailed Analysis," page 15.

The authors of this Congregational Conflict Type Indicator are committed to developing healthy congregations based on the (b) model of congregational interaction. If no more than 5% of total responses are located in section (a) or section (c), and at least ninety percent of total responses are located in section (b) your congregation may be viewed as being an exceptionally healthy congregational system in the way it manages conflict. If as many as fifteen percent of total responses fall into either section (a) or (c), your congregation merits further evaluation. If fewer than sixty percent of total responses are located in section (b) your congregation may benefit from more in-depth assistance from an outside professional conflict consultant. (Also use such a consultant to adapt the test to cultural groups valuing indirectness. Such persons will likely have few (b) answers.)

(a) responses point to a more erratic, hyperreactive response to disagreement. In general this means that members of the congregation overreact to difficult events in congregational life. Their emotions are loose and uncontrolled, and they have difficulty assessing the relative importance of different levels of distress. Further conversation or assistance may be indicated to learn how to respond to difficult situations in congregational life with less anxiety.

(b) responses point to a healthier, more balanced, whole-group process in response to disagreement. In general, this means that members of the congregation react appropriately to difficult events in congregational life. Their emotions are balanced and under control. They are able to respect one another and discern appropriate responses to a variety of crisis situations in congregational life.

(c) responses point to a more closed, underreactive response to disagreement. In general this means that members of the congregation underreact to difficult events in congregational life. Their emotions are tight and frozen, and joy is seldom expressed freely. Further conversation or assistance may be indicated to learn how to respond to difficult situations in congregational life with openness and integrity.

Further Steps You May Take

If your scores under (a) and (c) are less than fifteen percent this may indicate overall congregational health in terms of dealing with conflict issues. To learn more about how to become a stronger, healthier congregation, you may work through *Transforming Conflict in Your Church: A Practical Guide* (this manual) on your own as a leadership team, small group, or as a Bible study group.

If your scores under either (a) or (c) are greater than fifteen percent this may indicate that problems exist in the way your congregation manages conflict. We recommend that you secure counsel from your conference minister or other denominational officals about what steps are appropriate to improve congregational dynamics. Additional study materials and consulting organizations are described in Appendixes C and D of this manual.

A More Detailed Analysis

If you want a more detailed analysis of the five types of conflict that are discussed in *Transforming Conflict*, complete the following tables. Question numbers appear at the top of each table, and the three scoring options appear down the left side. Put a check mark in each of the squares which identifies how you scored your survey. Total the number of marks for each scoring option. If you have a significant number of marks in any (a) or (c) grid (more than 2 or 3), you need to take a look at that issue. It may indicate that this is one source of recurrent destructive conflict.

Interpersonal Relationships

Question	1	5	8	12	14	16	18	21	25	Total
(a)										
(b)										
(c)										

Communication/Information Sharing

Question	2	9	13	17	22	27	28	29	30	Total
(a)										
(b)										
(c)										

Decision Making

Question	1	7	10	13	17	24	25	30	32	Total
(a)										
(b)										
(c)										

Leadership Issues

Question	3	6	11	13	14	17	20	28	Total
(a)									
(b)									
(c)									

Boundaries Issues

Question	4	15	18	19	21	23	26	28	31	Total
(a)										
(b)										
(c)										
(d)										

Chapter One:

Understanding Conflict

Conflict is a part of everyday life. Whenever we have to adjust to a change, whether good or bad, we may find ourselves feeling blocked by someone else. The essence of conflict is that one person thinks another is preventing them from meeting their needs or goals.

By itself, conflict is neither good nor bad. But we can choose to deal with it constructively or destructively. Thus, the outcome of conflict resolution can be either good or bad. It can divide us, or it can strengthen us. It can be a doorway to growth, or a pit that entraps us. The danger in conflict is that we may move farther apart. The opportunity is that we can grow closer together.

Getting rid of conflict, as defined here, is impossible. In fact, we may not want to, especially if conflict can be an open door that brings about creative, constructive change. "Rocking the boat" or "upsetting the apple cart" (in other words, creating some kinds of conflict) is sometimes even beneficial. At the same time, limiting or managing the intensity of conflict is also important for preventing confusion, chaos, and even violence. We should never desire to create conflict, or engage in conflict, just for the sake of conflict. But when conflict—disagreement—can help us see things more clearly and bring about better decisions, it can be a helpful tool in accomplishing God's work.

In order to accomplish positive change through conflict, we need a fundamental shift in our thinking about conflict. The conflict we see around us—in the world, in our neighborhoods, and even in our churches—is often frightening. Some people talk about managing conflict, but it often manages us! But conflict can be transformed into an opportunity for growth and ultimately produce more authentic harmony.

This transformation takes place as all parties involved in the conflict seek to understand each other according to Matthew 18:15-20, even in the midst of intense disagreement. Conflicts are thus transformed from moments of division and destruction into opportunities for growth and greater cooperation.

How Do You Usually Talk About Solving Conflict?
____Avoiding conflict? (We walk away from it, letting the other person(s) win.)
____Resolving conflict? (We may seek a compromise, so everyone is somewhat satisfied.)
____Managing conflict? (We try to hold things together by any means possible, so things don't "fly apart.")
____Transforming conflict? (We find ways, in Christ, to turn disagreements into moments of growth and understanding, so we all can be more effective in our Christian lives, relationships, and ministries.)

What does the transformation of conflict involve?
There are times when change needs to take place at both the personal and organizational levels. We may continue to invite greater emotional and spiritual maturity, and learn new skills. It is important to invite healing in relationships and solve practical problems. We value harmony and pursue justice. We may lift up unity and affirm differences.

This manual offers some of the beginning steps in that transforming process, for those who care about congregations and find themselves in the midst of conflicts involving the body of Christ.

In this chapter we will introduce you to what conflict is and how it works. In chapter 2 you will learn how conflict escalates into fierce, storm-like proportions, and what you can do about it at different levels of intensity. Then chapter 3 will help you understand how to interpret the results of the Congregational Conflict Type Indicator (CCTI). Finally, chapters 4 and 5 will lead you through several ways of transforming conflict yourselves, as well as discerning when and how to get additional outside help.

What is conflict?

One definition of conflict states, "Conflict is an expressed struggle between at least two interdependent parties who perceive incompatible goals, scarce resources, and interference from others in achieving their goals." [1]

This definition points to several elements present in nearly all conflicts. The emphasis on perception is important, because it is difficult to see any point of view other than our own, especially in conflict. And while we know that "it takes two" to disagree, it is sometimes difficult to accept that the most creative and lasting solutions require input from everyone involved.

People have their own ways of, or images for, describing conflict. What is your experience? Finish this sentence: "For me, conflict is like _____."

The images or metaphors that may come to mind (dynamite, a game of chess, a hidden iceberg, etc.) reveal important things about the way we think and feel about conflict. They also provide clues to how we might go about transforming conflict in appropriate and effective ways.

TO DO:

If you want to understand more about how people in your church, fellowship, or group view conflict, take a few minutes for the following exercise. Complete the following sentence: "Conflict at (name of church, fellowship, or group) _____

_____ is like _____."

Or, instead of writing down the answer, draw a picture in the space below or on a separate sheet of paper to share with the group.

When everyone is finished, have each person briefly describe his or her word or picture, explaining the meaning behind the image. Then, as a group, try to explore some of the ways each image suggests you can work at conflict.

Christians and conflict

Christians are not immune to conflict. In fact, the strength of our convictions and our commitment to God seems to make conflict even more intense within the body of Christ. However, our ability to deal with conflict in the spirit of Jesus is one of the key factors in determining how effectively we minister in the church. Because we cannot eliminate conflict from our lives, we must discover the means for transforming potentially divisive conflicts into opportunities for growth and constructive change.

God's peace, called *shalom* in the Old Testament, is central to the gospel. Justice for parties who disagree with each other is an essential part of this true, biblical peace.

The Bible is like a kind of textbook in conflict studies. In it we find examples ranging from how not to deal with conflict (Abram in Egypt) to some extraordinary examples of creative conflict transformation (Solomon judging between the two women who claimed one baby). We discover a diversity of approaches, ranging from giving in to violent confrontation to joint partnering in seeking good solutions that work well for God's glory.

Conflict is transformed through many different means. They include:
- *Advocacy*—speaking out on behalf of another.
- *Facilitation/conciliation*—providing a safe environment in which persons in disagreement may speak together of their concerns with the help of a trusted third party. [2]
- *Mediation*—offering trained, professional guidance and a clear process for individuals who can no longer speak together positively about their disagreements.
- *Arbitration*—inviting trusted individuals outside the circle of disagreement to make decisions regarding the issues of disagreement for the parties.

Out of all these examples arises a way of peacemaking that is central to what it means to be God's people. At the very heart of the gospel is a message of repentance, forgiveness, reconciliation, and salvation. This is God's true *shalom* desired for all people.

In a church experiencing destructive conflict, someone may think or say, "The real problem here is that people are not right with God. If we really acted as Christians should, we wouldn't be in such a mess as this." The message in such a statement is that conflict is always sin. This viewpoint is understandable, because we do not always act skillfully in conflict and our experience of it is often negative and painful. While we often engage in sinful behaviors in the midst of conflict, conflict (disagreement with others) in itself is not sin. The biblical basis for this statement will become apparent in studying the next several pages.

TO DO:

Answer the question, When people in your congregation speak of conflict, what do they say?

_____

_____

_____

_____

Five Insights for Understanding Conflict

Here are five insights that provide a deeper understanding of conflict from the biblical texts.[3]

Insight no. 1:

Conflict is a normal part of life for all people, both in and out of the church.

Try to imagine a marriage or some other close relationship having no different points of view. While it may seem ideal for a short time, stagnation soon sets in. The result is no growth and a slow, gradual distancing that eventually turns the relationship cold.

While it seems obvious to us that too much conflict can be harmful, the opposite is also true. A church without a measure of healthy disagreement and conflict can become like salt that has lost its taste or a light hidden under a bushel basket (Matt. 5:13, 15).

God's creation, as described in Genesis, brought forth diversity in life. These God-given differences, as experienced from the time of creation until today, make for conflict in the body of Christ. The apostle Paul said, "When any of you has a grievance against another . . . ," not, "If any of you has a grievance against another . . ." (1 Cor. 6:1). Like Jesus, he assumed that the church would experience conflict. It affirms that we are a living body. Thankfully, we are given guidance for transforming conflict into a healthy part of our life together.

TO DO:

Look up the following Scriptures to see what they say about conflict as a normal part of life.

Romans 14:1-6, 10-12 _____

_____

_____

Galatians 2 _____

_____

_____

1 Corinthians 1 _____

_____

_____

Philippians 3 _____

_____

_____

Acts 6 and 15 _____

_____

_____

Insight no. 2:
Conflict becomes sinful when our responses to it are destructive, hurtful, abusive, or violent.

Conflict often occurs over issues that focus on behaviors with which we disagree. If the conflict turns into a contest between "us" and "them," "their" behavior is identified as sinful. But even people who feel they are "right" on the issue can treat others in very unloving ways. Being faithful to Christ involves more than taking the right stance on issues. It also requires engaging those with whom we disagree in positive, respectful dialogue.

TO DO:
Look up the following Scriptures to see what they say about *when* conflict becomes sinful.

Matthew 7:1-5 _____

_____

_____

John 8:1-11 _____

_____

_____

Romans 2:1-4 _____

_____

_____

Anger is not wrong! But it can turn into hate and even result in murderous acts (Gen. 4:7). Ephesians 4:26 teaches, "Be angry, but do not sin; do not let the sun go down on your anger." Anger is a natural human emotion, which occurs when we are offended or upset. Like any emotion, it will subside if we give it time, and common sense will return to us. Then we can make better decisions about how to handle the offense or upset feelings we had.

This may explain why Scripture says God became angry, and then later he "repented" of his anger (KJV), that is, God decided not to wreak vengeance on erring humankind. It simply underscores the truth that anger is a transitory emotion, and any decisions we make in an angry frame of mind will likely be the wrong ones. Anger and hostility can also indicate the presence of fear and pain. As such it can lead to hurtful responses by anyone threatened with the presence of such fear or pain.

Because anger is the initial emotional response to something that annoys you, Scripture teaches us to deal with the situation quickly (Eph. 4:26). Otherwise, the emotion can become entrenched in our psyche, and turn into hate. Hate colors our attitude toward everything in life, and causes us to act in ungodly ways. As God told Cain, when we don't deal with anger, sin lies crouching at the door, desiring to possess us (Gen. 4:7). The actions that surface because of bitterness and hatred are sinful, and can destroy, both others and ourselves.

But our actions in conflict don't have to add to the injury that may already have been experienced. This is especially true if we follow the teaching of Scripture as discussed above. In all matters we are commanded to "do to others as you would have them do to you" (Matt. 7:12). The apostle Paul provides a very practical application of this insight in 1 Corinthians 6:1-7 (in discussing Christians and lawsuits). This is perhaps one of the most ignored passages in many Christian groups.

Insight no. 3:
The Bible provides guidance for both attitude and process in dealing with conflict.

We share common bonds in Christ, and are admonished to speak the truth, be kind, humble, gentle, respectful, accountable, nonjudgmental, loving, and forgiving. Matthew 18:15-20 speaks to us about what to do when there is brokenness. Dealing with broken relationships is the business of the church. Bringing about forgiveness and healing is God's work, but it is the concern of the entire faith community. It is everybody's business.

Like Jesus, we are admonished to treat kindly those who live and believe differently than we. This does not mean compromising the gospel or ignoring our deepest convictions. But it does mean living by the "fruit of the Spirit" (Gal. 5:22-23), and humbly recognizing our own imperfect, sinful condition before God. Jesus showed his love for those with whom he disagreed. He made it very clear where he stood, always leaving the door open as a standing invitation for all to share in his vision and commitments.

God guides us in conflict. Not just by giving us practical steps for confronting others (Matt. 18:15-17), but by promising to be present with us in times of discord when healing and forgiveness are needed (Matt. 18:20).

TO DO:
Look up the following Scriptures to see what they say about managing our attitudes in conflict and the process of dealing with conflict.

Matthew 5:21-26 _____

_____

_____

Matthew 18:15-20 _____

_____

_____

1 Corinthians 13:4-7 _____

_____

_____

Galatians 6:1-5 _____

_____

_____

1 Peter 3:8, 16 _____

_____

_____

Insight no. 4:
Conflict can be used by God for learning, growth, and transformation.

We can come to know God more deeply in times of conflict. Conflict can damage relationships and tear apart community. But conflict can also be an opportunity, strengthening relationships and building up the body of Christ. How we approach conflict helps determine what its result will be. If we actively look for growth and illumination, we can find it.

Throughout the history of the church, God has spoken in the midst of conflict. We see this in the conflicts recorded in Acts 6 and 15, where fundamental truths about the participation of believers in the work of God's kingdom emerged.

Important creeds, doctrines, and even the formation of the scriptural canon emerged out of conflict. God is present with us and often speaks when Christians face conflict openly and honestly. While not every disagreement leads to "revelation," we may deny ourselves opportunities to hear God's voice if we avoid conflict or end it prematurely.

TO DO:
Look up the following Scriptures to see what they teach about God's guidance in the midst of conflict. Also, review the following events of history to see how conflict helped God's people discern his will. (A brief summary of each historical event is given in Appendix E.)

Acts 6 _____

_____

_____

Acts 15 _____

_____

_____

Council of Nicea _____

_____

_____

Martin Luther's Ninety-Five Theses _____

_____

_____

Conrad Grebel's Dispute with the City Council over Baptism _____

_____

_____

Vatican II _____

_____

_____

Insight no. 5:
As Christians, we seek not the absence of conflict (disagreement) but the presence of shalom.

Shalom is God's peace based on truth, mercy, and justice. It is embodied in love, forgiveness, reconciliation, and the restoration of right relationship with God and one another. Ron Kraybill, a well-known church mediator, says, "If you want to have less conflict, you should try to have more." He's not trying to stir up more conflict in the pews! What he means is, if you want to have less *harmful* conflict you should encourage open and honest disagreement while still treating others respectfully.

Restoring relationships broken in conflict requires (1) acknowledging the wrong we did and accepting responsibility for hurting the other (truth-telling); (2) the need for acceptance, letting go of past hurts, and a new beginning (mercy); (3) recognition of rights, the need for restructuring, and restitution (justice); (4) a sense of well-being (peace/*shalom*).

Genuine reconciliation, made possible by the cross, is both a horizontal and vertical experience. Peacemaking requires individual transformation (in relation to God) and the breaking down and crossing of social barriers (in relation to others). Our relationships with others have implications for our relationship with God, and even for our salvation. (See, for example, Matt. 5:23-24; 6:14-15; Isa. 58:4, 6-7; Amos 5:21, 23-24; Eph. 2:13-17; Mic. 6:6-8; 2 Cor. 5:17-21; Col. 3:12-15.)

TO DO:
Look up the following Scriptures to see what they say about finding *shalom* in the midst of conflict.

Genesis 14 _____

_____

_____

Psalm 85 _____

_____

_____

Ephesians 2:13-17 _____

_____

_____

2 Corinthians 5:17-21 _____

_____

_____

Amos 5:21-24 _____

_____

_____

Micah 6:6-8 _____

_____

_____

Matthew 5:23-24 _____

_____

_____

Matthew 6:14-15 _____

_____

_____

Matthew 23:23-24 _____

_____

_____

Colossians 3:12-15 _____

_____

_____

The "Stuff" of Conflict

Conflict can be complex. Issues and relationships often overlap. We need some ways to help us make sense out of what's going on when conflict occurs. In chapter 2, you will find a helpful overview of conflict levels for determining how serious your conflict may be (or if it is a conflict at all). Here we'll present two other ways for understanding the different shapes and forms in which conflict comes.

Types of conflict.

Some people have found it helpful to identify several different "types" of conflict as a way to better understand how to deal with conflict.

- Conflict can be experienced within yourself over matters of conscience or personal choice. This type of *intrapersonal* conflict may occur daily and vary in degree of severity.
- Conflict between two persons is usually referred to as *interpersonal* conflict and occurs over a wide range of issues in a variety of relationships. It also varies in intensity, from mild to violent.
- *Intragroup* conflict is a natural part of life together, whether there are conflicts within a family, committee, or a larger group (such as a church).
- Finally, disagreement between two interacting groups may result in *intergroup* conflict.

Dynamics within or between individuals or groups frequently overlap and may be present in any conflict.

TO DO:

Which type/s of conflict described on page 24 do you see occurring most often in your church?

_____

_____

_____

_____

Issues in conflict.

Even though the things we disagree about can seem almost endless, in reality there are only a limited number of issues that conflict can be about. In the pyramid diagram below, several kinds of conflict issues are identified.

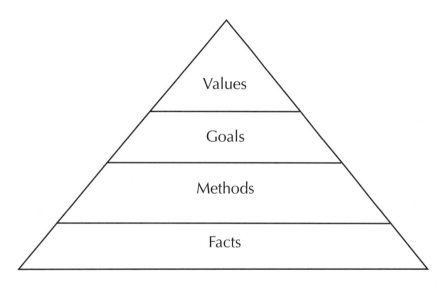

1. At the bottom are basic *facts* about events, behaviors, and resources that may come into dispute. Lack of information or miscommunication often contributes to such conflict. With some skill, they are easily recognized and readily resolved.

However, once a problem gets big enough facts become more of a hindrance than a help. In such cases the truth does not matter as much as each person's perception of it. What then becomes important is that we seek to understand each other's perception of the facts, and find a way to resolve the disagreement from that perspective.

2. Above that are the conflicts we experience over the *methods* we employ for achieving what we want in our life, work, and relationships. Our personal style, or way of responding to things around us, can be included here. People can be just as concerned about how something is dealt with (process) as they are about the issue (content) itself. That is, they may go along with something they don't like if they are treated respectfully.

Ignoring good process can become a source of conflict. While disagreement over process can be intense, it is not as difficult to deal with as issues at the next level up.

3. *Goals* frequently determine our direction in life. They are often established after much thought and effort, and are not easily changed. Almost all conflicts involve the perception of incompatible goals. People often do want different things and resent others whom they believe are interfering with them. A real disagreement over an issue of this type can quickly become a contest matter and may require outside help for resolution.

The ability to identify shared goals is one key to overcoming differences. Working together to identify and form clearly identified, shared goals can make it easier to work through disagreements over how to achieve the goals.

4. Above all other types of conflict, forming the capstone of our pyramid, is our sense of security, identity, and the *values* which underlie our purpose in life. These are the conflicts that are the most difficult to transform into a just peace, or *shalom*. Established over many years and tied to some of the most important things in life (like faith), conflict over issues of this kind are understandably the most difficult to work through.

Very often, as destructive conflicts become more intense, they are labeled, or framed, as differences in basic values, when they may more truthfully reflect concerns over goals, or even over methods.

For example, a disagreement about *how* to evangelize can be turned into a philosophical debate over the importance of certain types of mission programs. Or a debate over different styles of furnishings in a church remodeling program can be labeled as a desire for ornate worldly things at the expense of support for missions.

TO DO:

Which of the four types of conflict mentioned above do you see occurring most often in your church?

_____

_____

_____

_____

One Approach to Conflict Transformation

The place to begin conflict transformation is learning how to understand yourself and manage yourself better. Being aware of how you react in times of stress can open up choices you didn't know you had. Knowing yourself, and understanding and respecting the differences in others, can change your conflict behavior from knee-jerk reactions to purposeful responses. With skill and practice, you can anticipate conflict and become proactive.

One of the most familiar approaches to conflict transformation is in identifying five different strategies for dealing with conflict. They are (1) competition (or forcing), (2) collaboration, (3) compromise, (4) avoidance, and (5) accommodation. In the diagram below, each approach is located on a graph in relation to two factors: concern for personal goals (along the side) and concern for relationship (along the bottom).

The graph shows that Forcing (competition in problem solving) has a high goals orientation, but a low interest in maintaining relationships; Collaborating has a high goals orientation and also a high interest in maintaining relationships, etc.

CONNECTION BETWEEN GOALS AND RELATIONSHIPS

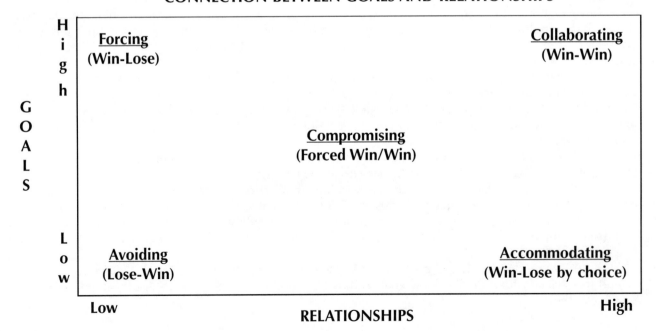

Most people use all of these strategies at one time or another. While collaboration might seem like the best approach to healthy conflict transformation, each approach has advantages and disadvantages.

For example, if you almost get into an accident with a stranger while driving your car, you probably won't take the time to pull over and talk things out with him in a collaborative manner. You'll probably just drive on (an avoidance approach). In the same way, if you're ever on an airplane that has an emergency, you won't expect the captain to come into the cabin and ask if anyone wants to help him or her figure out a mutually agreeable course of action for solving the problem (a collaborative approach). You expect him or her to take action on his or her own (a "forcing" approach)! But in developing an evangelism strategy in the church, collaboration might be highly appropriate.

TO DO:

Here's an activity to help you understand the five approaches to conflict transformation more fully.

Think about some real-life situations in which each of the five conflict strategies would be appropriate. Name specific behaviors (e.g., persuasion, negotiation, withdrawal) that might go along with each strategy and give examples of a conflict where each approach would be appropriate.

Accommodation _____

_____

_____

Avoidance _____

_____

_____

Competition / Forcing _____

_____

_____

Compromise _____

_____

_____

Collaboration _____

_____

_____

As you think about this you may discover that you seem to use one approach to conflict significantly more than others. Each of us has a preferred conflict style—a characteristic way of responding to others and things around us. The more you can learn about your own preferences in dealing with conflict, the better you will be prepared to make choices for transforming that conflict in healthy ways.

If you're interested, see Appendix B, page 53, for reference to conflict styles instruments which can help you assess your usual style of response.

TO DO:

Which conflict transformation style do you prefer when you experience conflict?

_____

_____

_____

_____

In this chapter we have tried to give you several ways of making sense of a complicated part of life—conflict. We hope you will reflect on conflicts in which you are involved, or those of which you are aware. But reflection and self-awareness only go so far. The real key to dealing effectively with conflict is in developing skills that help you and others function at your best, and keep you open to discerning God's will.

The rest of this manual is designed to increase your understanding of conflict (an analytic skill), present some practical ideas for dealing with conflict (process skills), and provide some suggestions for those times when you feel "in over your head" (assessment skills).

Pontius' Puddle

Chapter Two:
Escalating Levels of Conflict[1]

Viewers watching the Wizard of Oz can see storm clouds looming on the horizon long before Dorothy can. Those who have previously experienced the escalating stages of a summer storm are not surprised as balmy summer air changes quickly into a destructive tornado.

What are the stages of a developing church storm, and what are telltale signs of the escalating friction pointing to a church conflict tornado?

Level One: Disagreements are a normal part of everyday life together. Healthy groups see them as *problems to solve*, not as differences that may divide the group. They are like white, fluffy clouds lazily dotting the horizon on a warm, mid-summer day.

Those individuals who experience the disagreement speak directly with each other about the disagreement, and discover that a potential storm is transformed into united energy for mission. They may disagree on a precise definition of the problem, and may also have differing views for a solution. But they are spiritually connected, and work diligently together in search of mutually satisfying options to resolve the situation.

They share appropriate information about the issue with each other in open and trusting ways. They own their own different feelings, share them with each other, and care for one another redemptively. They respect one another's views, and negotiate their differences so each feels respected and cared for (Phil. 2:2-4).

- How frequently does your congregation transform disagreements into unified action by talking about the issues in this way? Check up on yourselves by naming three recent disagreements or conflicts you have faced together, and determine how closely you followed the suggestions given above. (Give a name to each conflict, and briefly summarize your responses to it.)

Conflict No. 1: _____

_____

_____

Conflict No. 2: _____

_____

_____

Conflict No. 3: _____

_____

_____

Level Two: If one individual, or a subgroup in the larger group, begins to feel their needs and concerns are being overlooked, they begin to sense an uncomfortable *disagreement* with others. White, fluffy summer clouds begin to turn dark on the horizon! Those individuals who do not feel "heard" begin to talk to their closest friends, who will listen to and agree with them. They may then tell others with whom they disagree that "a lot of people"—or even "everyone" has the same view as they do.

As the disagreement sharpens information becomes vague, unclear, and incomplete. People share what information they do have only with those who agree with them. They begin to guard their feelings, and often deny that there really is a problem. They trivialize other persons' viewpoints, sometimes even joking about them in critical ways. The differences that do exist are debated, rather than negotiated, often resulting in splitting hairs over technicalities and fine points.

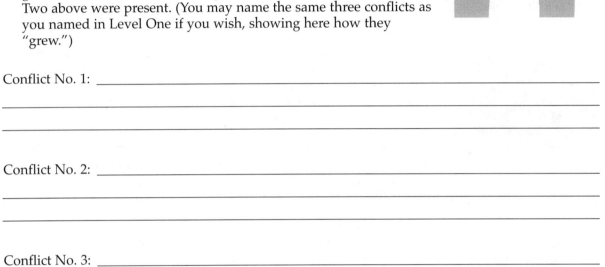

- How frequently do some of the behaviors mentioned in Level Two find their place in your congregation, as you seek to deal with your disagreements? Check up on yourselves by naming below three recent disagreements or conflicts that have occurred in your congregation, and determine how many of the behaviors described in Level Two above were present. (You may name the same three conflicts as you named in Level One if you wish, showing here how they "grew.")

Conflict No. 1: _____

_____

_____

Conflict No. 2: _____

_____

_____

Conflict No. 3: _____

_____

_____

As a Level Two disagreement escalates people within the organization become less and less able to work together clearly and objectively. Although some may try to become "peacemakers," they usually tend to promote the view they believe to be right, encouraging others to "fall in line." Instead of bringing greater harmony, this approach simply escalates the tension.

Level Three: If individuals cannot return to a Level One objective discussion, the uneasy spirit of a Level Two disagreement develops into a *contest*. Dark clouds fill the sky and fierce winds begin to blow. People begin to take sides, each led ultimately by one or more spokespersons. Accusations escalate, and information becomes distorted and one-sided. Feelings become tense and tight, "justified" on the basis of the injustices of others. The views of people with whom they disagree are rejected outright, and the differences that already exist heighten and distort the truth even more.

- How frequently do some of the behaviors mentioned in Level Three find their place in your congregation, as you seek to deal with your disagreements? Check up on yourselves by naming below three recent disagreements / conflicts that have occurred in your congregation, and determine how many of the behaviors described in Level Three above were present. (You may name the same three conflicts as you named in Level Two if you wish, showing here how they "grew.")

Conflict No. 1: _____

_____

_____

Conflict No. 2: _____

_____

_____

Conflict No. 3: _____

_____

_____

To avoid Level Three conflict individuals need to reconnect spiritually and emotionally. They can do this by utilizing the spiritual disciplines of prayer, worship, and fellowship. They also need to transform the "tornado" into summer calm by again returning to the Level One characteristics of problem solving, speaking directly to one another with objectivity, respect, and courtesy. They must evidence a clear desire to resolve their differences justly and fairly.

If a Level Three conflict is not avoided it increases in intensity until it becomes virtually impossible for anyone within the church to help those involved achieve a fair and just resolution of the issues. Even if that individual were able to remain objective and fair, few people in the center of the conflict would perceive him or her as being so. The most consistently helpful way to keep this level of conflict from escalating to a storm of Level Four proportions, with the inevitable loss of members and perhaps even the loss of the pastor or other leaders, is for the congregation to get outside help.

(Unfortunately, if a conflict is allowed to escalate to this level, it is extremely hard to trust anyone outside the congregation, either, to provide the help that is needed. It is also much harder to admit that help is needed. For both of these reasons, it is better to get help earlier, as the conflict moves from Level Two into Level Three.)

The first step in getting outside help is to contact the area denominational supervisor (conference minister, overseer, district superintendent, etc.). If they are unable to help resolve the crisis at this level (and many times it is even too late for that type of assistance), they can provide names of outside individuals and organizations who can help. (See chapter 5 for more guidance on appropriate ways of seeking outside help.)

In order to resolve the crisis successfully and transform a Level Three storm into harmony again, emotions must be relaxed, justice for all must be sought, and fellowship must be restored. The congregation must be returned to a healthy Level One, problem-solving spirit regarding the issues over which they disagree.

Level Four: If the polarization of a Level Three conflict is not resolved successfully, it will inevitably evolve into a full-blown *church fight*. Lightning begins to flash, thunderclaps further disturb the uneasy atmosphere, and rain, sleet or hail begins to cover the landscape.

People who are by now hopelessly locked into their own view of things will warn of "dire consequences" if things don't change. Some will cease attending services, some will begin to attend elsewhere ("only until the storm subsides," they say), and others will threaten to leave. People begin to speak of the actions of those they disagree with as sinful, and often lose control of their emotional poise. Differences are seen in terms of absolutes, and labeled as right (the way I see it) and wrong (the way you see it).

• How frequently do some of the behaviors mentioned in Level Four find their place in your congregation, as you seek to deal with your disagreements?

Check up on yourselves by naming below three recent disagreements / conflicts that have occurred in your congregation, and determine how many of the behaviors described in Level Four above were present. (You may name the same three conflicts as you named in Level Three above if you wish, showing here how they "grew.")

Conflict No. 1: _____

_____

_____

Conflict No. 2: _____

_____

_____

Conflict No. 3: _____

_____

_____

It is usually at this stage of a conflict that congregational leadership gives up trying to solve the conflict on their own and chooses to call in outside help. As outside mediators and/or consultants begin to work with leadership and congregational members, the outside helper often discovers that many congregational members desire to put forward their own diagnosis of and solution for the problems, and warn that if certain things don't happen they, too, may leave.

By this time it is extremely difficult to avoid losses. It is often possible, however, for a trained mediator or consultant to help minimize the storm damage and slowly assist the congregation's return to transformation and wholeness.

The extent to which this is possible often depends upon four factors: (1) the commitment level of the congregation and its leadership to accept changes in the way they manage conflict, (2) the amount of energy which they are willing to devote to appropriate levels of reconciliation and restoration, (3) the resourcefulness of the consultant(s) and congregational leadership, and (4) the financial resources which are made available for the reconciliation process.

Actually, once a congregation finds itself in a Level Three conflict, there is no alternative but to expect a diversion of financial resources away from primary ministry. Invariably substantial proportions of offering income will be lost at Levels Three and Four, through restricted giving patterns, loss of members, and the costs associated with searching for and moving in a new pastor. Seldom does the current pastor survive a Level Four conflict.

(Actually, the beginnings of these patterns are found in Level Two already, and can be an early warning sign for the treasurer who is trained to look for such signs. Any regular giver who suddenly stops giving, or diverts his giving, is in need of care, and not necessarily because of the identified conflict. Regular giving is often one of the first recognizable casualties in church conflict. Apathy in fellowship and service is another.)

Securing the services of a competent professional conflict resolution mediator or consultant early in the conflict may be the *least* expensive way to deal with the crisis. These efforts can most effectively transform a potentially devastating storm into renewed energy for ministry.

Conflict resolution mediators or consultants provide several important services for the congregation in a Level Three or Level Four conflict storm.

• They can reduce anxiety by making it possible for everyone to be heard.
• They can assist in generating accurate, objective information about the conflict issues.

• They can assist congregational members and leaders in working through a fair and just approach to reconciliation and problem solving.

If the conflict issues are not resolved adequately at Level Four, one of two things may happen. (1) Some members may leave (often including the pastor). (2) The storm may pass, the sun come out again, and everything may appear to be resolved. In reality, however, it will only be a matter of time before another storm appears on the horizon.

Level Five: On the other hand, even if some members leave, others who refuse to leave may continue the now *intractable* (unsolvable) stormy contest until they feel vindicated. If this is true of more than one subgroup involved in the conflict, tension can escalate even farther. After the rain and hail there is a brief calm, followed by a more ferocious tornado than before.

Individuals threaten each other, but refuse to leave until the "truth" (their view) is vindicated. Information gels into ideology, with opponents being viewed as agents of evil, needing to be rooted out. Emotions become so hardened they appear to be nonexistent. People feel obliged to defame, often abusively, the views of others. Different points of view become, in effect, the objects of a "holy war"[2] to defend the truth and stamp out evil. This behavior may even be true of some who left the church at Level Four, but feel compelled to continue the battle for truth from the outside.

• How frequently do some of the behaviors mentioned in Level Five find their place in your congregation, as you seek to deal with your disagreements? Check up on yourselves by naming below three recent disagreements / conflicts that have occurred in your congregation, and determine how many of the behaviors described in Level Five above were present. (You may name the same three conflicts as you named in Level Four above if you wish, showing here how they "grew.")

Conflict No. 1: _____

_____

_____

Conflict No. 2: _____

_____

_____

Conflict No. 3: _____

_____

_____

At this highest and most deadly level of conflict, repentance on the part of everyone involved in the conflict is of the highest priority. By this time everyone has sinned, in attitude, word, or deed. Repentance is the only way to transform a Level Five storm into spiritual wholeness.

In addition to repentance, assistance will be needed from denominational officials, mediators, consultants, and spiritual resource persons to return the congregation to normalcy once again.

If this is not possible, the only other solution may be to secure competent, professional assistance in dividing the church into two separate congregations, or in disbanding the group entirely.

The purpose for seeking outside help here is to assist those who are left in the congregation make these changes in a positive manner. It is important to inflict as little additional spiritual damage as possible and find some degree of spiritual healing for new beginnings.

For more assistance in determining what level of conflict may be occurring in your congregation, see Appendix A (page 51).

Chapter Three:

Systems Failures and How to Correct Them

Introduction

The church is not only an organization. It is a living organism. As Paul noted, Jesus Christ is its head, and the members are its body. It is a complex system, just as our bodies are.

When we study the workings of the human body, we see that it is a fragile, yet adaptable system. It is able to ward off disease and avoid injury. Yet just as our bodies become sick or disabled, the church's system can also become ill.

In this chapter we'll look at the results of the Congregational Conflict Type Indicator (CCTI) which you may already have completed (pages 9-12). If you have, it will help you take the temperature of your congregation—give it a "physical." Are all the bodily systems working well? Are there areas of concern which need attention? Is the congregation "eating right, getting enough exercise, and enough sleep"? Is your church body operating at its peak performance? Is it taking care of "illnesses" early, before they become serious?

When you get sick you don't always call an ambulance or go to the emergency room. Most illnesses are common, and you can take care of them yourself. "Drink plenty of fluids and get plenty of rest" is the standard prescription for the common cold. Often ailments in church systems need no more than that general type of attention. Sometimes, however, a physical illness hangs on, not responding well to home remedies. We need to pay attention when an illness worsens, or when puzzling symptoms crop up. That's when we go see the doctor.

1. Interpersonal Relationships

(CCTI questions relating to this section include numbers 1, 5, 8, 12, 14, 16, 18, 21, 25.)

Conflict always begins with some *change* in our relationships or environment. Change is confusing. It may lead to disagreement, or it may just cause confusion. We never know if it will lead to an "illness" or not.

Human beings usually don't like having to adjust to change, and the standard response is to get through the confusion as quickly as possible. The most usual way of getting through it is to blame someone else for causing the change. Once we know who is at fault, the change is not so confusing and is more easily dealt with.

For example, a youth leader makes some last-minute changes in the youth travel schedule for a retreat. This adjustment may confuse the youth as well as their parents. The confusion is uncomfortable for some of them. They say to themselves, and to each other, "Who does he think he is, changing the schedule at the last minute like that without asking us? Don't we count for anything around here?" That relieves some of the confusion. The youth and parents have addressed their confusion by deciding that the youth leader is insensitive and uncaring.

A major ministry problem

Notice that no *direct communication* has occurred here. If the youth or parents had asked the youth leader about it, he could have explained the reason for the schedule change, and apologized for failing to explain it to them adequately in the first place. That would have dispelled the feelings of confusion in a better way, and restored a spirit of harmony and respect.

When some unexplained or abrupt change confuses us, it is best to resolve the confusion by direct communication with the person(s) involved, rather than by making assumptions or insinuations about attitudes or motives.

This same problem shows up in congregational meetings. Since conflict is often considered bad, *questioning* the wisdom of anyone's recommendation in a meeting may also be interpreted as bad. The leaders of this type of congregation are accustomed to presenting recommendations that are adopted without much comment by the congregation. Such an approach does not allow for evaluation and the healthy interchange of ideas, which strengthens congregations.

People who feel imposed upon by such a decision also feel they have the right to *ignore* the decision. A common example is a congregational decision to spend money on some project, only to have a significant number of people who participated in the decision fail to support the project financially. This causes hurt for the persons interested in the project, since they may have understood silence to mean support. A congregation that experiences silence in meetings cannot interpret that silence as agreement. It is much better to work hard at striving toward consensus in open, trusting dialogue.

Another major ministry problem

Circles of influence also tend to create confusion, especially when people in those circles keep information to themselves, or don't interact effectively with a broad range of views in the congregation. These circles of influence, often called "cliques," can show up in extended families, small-group organizations, specialized interest groups (such as a Mom's Club or a golfing foursome), tightly knit Bible study and prayer groups, and many others. Sometimes they really do try to control outcomes of decision making, although other times they simply create the illusion that they seek to control outcomes.

The way to avoid such confusion is to develop a healthy "cross-stitching"[1] pattern of communication, where members of such natural circles of friendship also interact openly and often with a wide range of persons not a part of their special group, and keep information flowing naturally in all directions.

Differing levels of desire for *intimacy*, with its accompanying problems of *confidentiality*, can also cause relational confusion. Some people prefer to maintain a few very close and intimate friendships, and tend to expect those friends to keep much of what they share very confidential. Others maintain a wide and diverse array of friendships, sharing almost anything of a personal nature with anyone who happens to pass by. There are no secrets with them.

How confidences are respected in congregations where members have differing views of intimacy and confidentiality presents definite questions of boundaries. They must continually be worked at with respect for all individuals.

Other ministry problems

Personality clashes are a natural part of the human scene, just as certain foods and medications create confusion in the natural body (e.g., allergic reactions). To some degree such personality clashes cannot be avoided. They can be managed, however, just as the intake of food and medications can be monitored and managed.

A church's conflict resolution style is partly determined by the *behavior of the members toward one another* when a conflict arises. When a disagreement becomes public, or at least noticeable, some church members condemn those making waves. Since conflict is seen by some as bad, anyone involved in it must also be bad. The message is that conflict must not be allowed to exist. The attitude is, "Get over it quickly and let's hear no more of it." Other church members react to conflict by staying away from those involved. Conflict is dirty, they feel, and they don't want to get any of it on themselves.

An effective church transforms conflict by first supporting the integrity of the unity of the body of Christ, and not destroying those relationships. It also supports an open process for dealing with conflicts.

If church members know that conflict is normal, and that members of the body stand ready to help them through it, they are much more likely to resolve their differences in an effective way. A church which has good conflict transformation processes and an atmosphere which accepts conflict as a normal part of life will be much better prepared for the serious conflicts which come around once every generation or so.

TO THINK ABOUT:

Which of the following cause difficulties in relationships in your congregation?

☐ Communication problems
☐ Circles of influence
☐ Confidentiality problems
☐ Personality clashes
☐ Lack of open and honest evaluation
☐ Acceptance of differences among members
☐ Other _____

Which is the most problematic? What steps can you take right now to deal with the issues that cause relational problems in your congregation?

2. Communication/Information Sharing

(CCTI questions relating to this section include numbers 2, 9, 13, 17, 22, 27, 28, 29, 30.)

Information flow can be viewed as the lifeblood of congregational systems. A healthy flow keeps the various members and organs connected to the heart of church life and to one another. In a healthy system, information moves smoothly along the organizational stream, through the designated channels, with proper timing, and in appropriate amounts. It nourishes the body and helps carry away its waste materials.

In contrast, *lack of adequate communication* flow may leave uninformed members feeling undernourished, stale, or cut-off. One writer has likened this kind of secrecy to the plaque in an organization's arteries. Only the inner few receive the benefit of the communication stream, and the limited material coming through may be less than pure. As broader circulation wanes, parts of the body begin to atrophy and may even cease to function at all, with the entire body slowly and silently grinding to a halt.

At the other extreme, *too much information* or the wrong kind of information can overload the system. Members may feel overwhelmed by a constant flow of inadequately processed data, or may be confused by public sharing of private matters. The wild or erratic pumping of the heart may be felt throughout the body. Perhaps one or more areas of the body may become injured; circulatory vessels may break and bleed. Worried members may wonder if a stroke or hemorrhage is imminent.

So what *is* the proper rate of information flow? Some general guidelines can help keep the channels free of plaque and regulate the stream in healthy ways:

- General public information should be shared in a variety of formats, to meet different members' needs and interests.
- Oral announcements, short bulletin or newsletter updates, and availability of lengthier written reports and minutes for those seeking more content are also important.

Every church has a particular *method for communicating information* about congregational life.

- Announcements during the worship service, a weekly bulletin, monthly newsletter, and bulletin board notices are the most common methods used.
- Sometimes special meetings may be called to provide information on larger projects.
- Smaller congregations may have a telephone chain.
- E-mail is becoming more common for some congregations.

The ways in which you circulate information say something about how you value openness and good communication.

If information has to filter out through the grapevine, most people will understand that feedback is not wanted, and that those in charge will impose decisions on the majority. Churches that only communicate information through official documents are sending the same message. A church which values open communication will provide information through a variety of methods that invite questions and feedback. (The grapevine works differently in indirect cultures.) [2]

Some churches have *leaders* who don't believe they should have (or share) *strong opinions*. Whether the church's corporate personality encourages leadership of the weather vane variety, or whether the individual leader is just built that way, a leader who expresses no opinions keeps everyone else guessing and increases the confusion in the church system. It is important for the leader/s to express their point of view, without necessarily demanding that everyone subscribe to it.

Many churches don't know how to share information about controversial or conflict issues. Information about issues over which there is disagreement should be shared *openly without casting blame*. Congregational members should be helped to focus on the issues rather than on the personalities closest to the issues.

As the significance or tension of an issue goes up, it is helpful to move toward the anxiety with more (not less) opportunities for well-facilitated sharing and dialogue across different perspectives. Large- and small-group forums may be helpful for processing important information and identifying steps for further study, evaluation, and eventual decision making.

Special consideration must be given to sensitive information about church staff or members, to avoid the extremes of undue secrecy and/or simply "letting it all hang out."

Information of a solely *personal* nature should be shared by the affected person in the forum of their choosing: in one-on-one meetings, care groups, public prayer times, etc., and should be shared by others only at that individual's direction.

Information affecting *congregational life* should be shared first with those charged to address such issues—elders, the pastor-congregation relations committee, personnel chair, etc. This forum should discern appropriate steps for processing the information, seeking outside help as needed.

Persons directly affected by the issue should be informed at such times and in such detail as needed to address their legitimate concerns, always balancing the competing values of openness and confidentiality as appropriate to each level of information sharing.

TO THINK ABOUT:

Which of the following cause difficulties in communication in your congregation?

- ❏ Lack of adequate information
- ❏ Too much information
- ❏ Poor methods of communication
- ❏ Leaders who are too vocal about their personal views
- ❏ Leaders who are not clear enough about their personal views
- ❏ Conflict information shared in a way that focuses blame on individuals
- ❏ Other _____

3. Decision Making

(CCTI questions relating to this section include numbers 1, 7, 10, 13, 17, 24, 25, 30, 32.)

Which is the most problematic? What steps can you take right now to deal with the issues which cause communication problems in your congregation?

If communication is the lifeblood of the congregational body, decision making is how that "blood" gets utilized for sustaining growth and developing new programs. Like growth in organic life, decision making is a process, not a single or isolated event. A steady track record of well-executed decisions strengthens the life of the organization, giving it a solid operational foundation, just as regular aerobic exercise strengthens the human heart.

The first and probably the most important decision-making task is *goal-setting*. Athletes don't just start training; they first determine what races they want to win, and then train accordingly. It is no different in the church. The best plans are those that are developed with specific goals that can be accomplished. In other words, we make plans to accomplish goals, rather than making plans because that's what churches do.

After goals have been adequately thought through and owned by the whole congregation, *initial planning* is important before the activity commences. Unless the whole church is accustomed to spontaneous activity, just jumping in and doing it doesn't work well, and creates a lot of unnecessary tension and confusion.

Several guidelines are important in initial planning.

- The right group must be given the appropriate amount of authority to develop an action plan.
- The congregation must be kept informed at the appropriate level, and must be invited to provide feedback to the planning group.
- Final agreement on the plan of action must occur before the plan is carried out.
- Implementation must be under the supervision of the person or persons to whom the congregation entrusts such responsibility.
- Even after the activity begins, ongoing interactive feedback is important between leaders and followers.

Decision making often requires making smaller, step-by-step decisions along the way. Even when structures are clear, congregational leaders at times may rush into decision making, skipping key steps and input along the way. At other times, they may avoid making program decisions at all, putting off resolution until few healthy channels remain open.

When choices may significantly impact a congregation's future, like changing the constitution or addressing membership issues, the pacing and structure of the decision-making process become all the more critical. The exact process to be followed and the issues to be addressed should be agreed upon up front—at least printed in an agreed upon agenda. Then a variety of options should be solicited and evaluated openly and honestly, before selecting a solution that addresses as many of the interests and concerns of the membership as possible.

There is a tendency for some churches to drive away those persons involved in conflict disagreements surrounding decision-making issues. For them, dealing with different views in an effective way is so difficult that some people who are a part of the weaker or less well-connected side simply leave in frustration. Other churches spend so much energy on decision making that little else happens. Balance is the goal.

An effective church, focused on wholeness in ministry, prefers to work through conflict rather than drive some people away. While there is danger in honestly encountering such a crisis, the opportunity for conflict transformation is far greater.

As the decision is *implemented*, follow-up reporting will continue this sense of ownership and prompts greater cooperation in the implementation of decisions at the other end. Pretending there is no issue—or trying to "slip one past them"—are both recipes for disaster. Most people can live with even tough decisions, as long as there has been opportunity for genuine input and ongoing information flow.

The final healthy decision-making step is the discipline of regular ministry and program *evaluation*. Ministry and program evaluation structures need to be well designed and systematic, not simply reactive responses to personnel crises. Nor should they occur primarily at contract renewal time.

Plans for evaluation processes may include:

- Clear, up-to-date expectations about who needs to be involved in what decisions (pastor, elders, deacons, church council, whole congregation, etc.).

- Clear information about what constitutes the "decision rule" in a given context (e.g., consensus, majority, two-thirds, authority of office).
- Determination if the group actually followed the authorized channels.
- Determination if the group implemented the plans as originally laid out.

In some cases such an evaluation may require the use of an independent, outside process coordinator, so the evaluation is truly an objective exercise.

Clearly, leaders have an important role to play as process facilitators in congregational decision-making. Their role in defining and influencing substantive choices facing the congregation is explored in the section on Leadership, which follows.

TO THINK ABOUT:

At which of the following stages of decision making do difficulties occur in your congregation?

❏ Goal-setting
❏ Initial planning
❏ Implementation
❏ Evaluation
❏ Other _____

4. Leadership

(CCTI questions relating to this section include numbers 3, 6, 11, 13, 14, 17, 20, 28.)

Which is the most problematic? What steps can you take right now to deal with the issues that cause decision-making problems in your congregation?

There are at least three types of leaders in most congregations: pastoral staff, lay officers, and unofficial lay leaders. They have different roles, and because of that may have different ways of exerting their influence.

A pastor is set apart for particular types of leadership roles, which may vary somewhat among congregations and within pastoral teams. But some pastoral roles are fairly universal.

The pastor is usually called to be a prophetic voice, speaking in God's name. Often he or she serves as a counselor or comforter. At times the pastor is asked to be a facilitator. At other times the pastor becomes a business manager, personnel director, or program administrator.

A Mennonite Polity for Ministerial Leadership says this about pastoral leadership: "Ministers maintain a leadership style that is gentle and gracious but firm. Persons in pastoral ministry empower congregational members rather than seeking to be center stage. Differences will likely occur from time to time; nevertheless, it is expected that persons in pastoral ministry will speak well of the congregation and other congregational leaders where he/she serves." [3]

Besides pastors, congregations have *lay members who are selected for official leadership* positions in the church structure. It is common for these positions to rotate, and for many different people to hold them over time. They are responsible for helping the church fulfill its program functions.

Every church also has *unofficial leaders*. These are the people who, whether elected to office or not, *have the respect of congregational members,* and therefore often have more influence on the outcomes of decision making than does the elected leadership or the pastor. Some congregations are actually controlled by one or two family groups, who sometimes never relinquish real power.

A problem many congregations have is that leadership responsibility and authority have been separated. Official leaders have responsibility, but often they can only exercise authority with the blessing of these behind-the-scene decision-makers. Where this situation exists, it is important to be aware of this dynamic and work with it so it doesn't create unnecessary congregational conflict.

It is common, for instance, for churches to install young leaders in positions of responsibility, while the real authority for decisions and the financial resources to implement them remains with their parents' generation. Decisions that are never implemented and frustration are the result.

All leaders have several responsibilities in common. They are:

1. Maintain an *open congregational process* in decision making. This includes keeping the congregation adequately informed, openly receiving counsel and advice, informing the congregation of different strands of opinion, explaining how and why decisions were made, and remaining open for ongoing evaluation and input.

2. *Share responsibility*. The congregationally based view of church requires that we all work together as team members. No one person has the right to make or carry out decisions without shared input from others. Besides distributing the power and work responsibility, this approach also ensures that the congregation will be better served in the long run.

3. *Do not blame or cast shame on others* for decisions and plans which did not work out. People acting in good faith do not generally engage in a project or make a decision for the purpose of failing or hurting others. Those who give of their time to serve the Lord do so out of a heart of love and dedication to God. When efforts fail those who suffered loss need the reassurance and love of the whole church, not the attacks and accusations of others.

4. *Evaluate, evaluate, always evaluate*. Evaluation should commence before the plan or idea is put into operation. It should continue while the decision is carried out, and should occur again after it has been concluded.

Evaluation is not for the purpose of criticizing, but to help us improve in our service to Christ and the family of God. Evaluation should not focus on individuals but on approaches, plans, and outcomes. Did the group achieve its goal? To what extent? How could it have been done better?

5. *Maintain a sense of good humor*. It is easy, in the intensity of trying to accomplish a program, to become so involved in achieving the immediate goal that one loses sight of the ultimate goal. That ultimate goal must always be serving God and God's people. Nothing is so important that it's worth losing a good sense of humor over it. A good sense of humor is a wonderful antidote to taking something or yourself too seriously and possibly failing for trying too hard. (Even Jesus maintained such a healthy balanced sense of humor!)

6. Finally, leaders must *stay on top of things*—always keeping at least one-half step ahead of the process. That includes thinking ahead, planning ahead, and networking with enough people so you remain aware of and can keep ahead of the pace. It is better to be ready with information about other options and their potential impact than to be surprised by unanticipated problems.

Many other ideas for good leadership also exist. Several are summarized in the brief article, "Conflict Management for Leaders: Some Principles," page 253, in *Mediation and Facilitation Training Manual*, 4th edition.[4]

Many times pastors are expected to be the conflict fixers of the congregation. They are expected to straighten out those who need it, and keep everyone appraised of their Christian duties.

In reality, the pastor must serve the entire church, and is best able to do so when not aligned with any faction, or not expected to serve as the mediator between conflicted individuals or subgroups in the church. It is often better for other members of the congregation to be the conflict managers, so that the minister can pastor everyone.

The pastor can be the catalyst for getting a process started, but is not the best person to facilitate it. A pastor trying to facilitate a conflict process will rapidly come to be viewed by both sides as being on "the other side."

Unofficial leaders lack the visible authority to intervene publicly, and are usually aligned with one faction or another. Therefore, they also are not the best suited for dealing with conflict in the church.

For this reason **the work of conflict transformation is best done by lay officeholders**. It is their responsibility, and they should be given the authority to work with the conflict issues of the church. Healthy, appropriate lay leadership needs to be recognized and supported in any conflict transformation process, whether the work is done internally or with the help of an outside consultant or mediator.

How the lay leadership works with conflict will be closely scrutinized by congregational members on all sides of the issue, and will be key to healthy conflict transformation. It is unlikely that the official leaders of a congregation will have much experience dealing with serious conflict or will feel adequate in doing so. Severe conflict events are usually farther apart than the length of time official lay leaders stay in office.

Ideally, congregations will address leadership development in this area through regular, proactive training and orientation of new leaders prior to their tenure in office. This includes skill-building, as well as awareness of additional resources available in the conference, region, and denomination.

People with training and experience in conflict transformation work at resolving their conflicts at earlier stages of stress than others. A trained and experienced person sticks with their confusion and frustration longer, and resolves it by directly communicating with the other person(s) involved. That practice by itself transforms conflicts at an earlier stage. (The foundation for such a plan exists in the Mennonite Church official statement, "Agreeing and Disagreeing in Love"—see chapter 4 for a summary of the document.)

Another proactive, leadership-oriented way to avoid severe, destructive conflict is by developing a congregational conflict management plan which everyone understands, before serious conflict arises. By using the plan faithfully in many small conflicts, these good practices will become natural to the congregation and fall into place more easily in severe conflicts.

Leaders have a responsibility to model good communication. As the practices suggested in this manual (and other resources) are used well by proactive leaders, the congregation will likely find itself in good health most of the time. It will also be better prepared for those times when serious conflicts threaten.

Trained and experienced leaders also have a better sense of when they need outside help, and have a plan for getting it. Part of good leadership is knowing when a situation is beyond your ability to manage it.

The time to first discuss bringing in a consultant is not when the church is polarized. This option needs to be part of the congregation's overall plan, so that official leaders have both the responsibility and authority to call for help when needed. How to assess the need for and seek outside assistance are discussed more fully in chapter 5.

TO THINK ABOUT:

Which of the following cause difficulties in leadership in your congregation?

❏ The relationship between the pastor, lay leaders, and the unofficial leaders of the congregation
❏ A closed congregational process in decision making
❏ Criticism, blaming, and shaming
❏ Poor or no evaluation
❏ Getting too serious about a program or project (not maintaining a good sense of humor)
❏ Leadership not being on top of things
❏ Other _____

Which is the most problematic? What steps can you take right now to deal with the issues that cause leadership problems in your congregation?

5. Boundaries

(CCTI questions relating to this section include numbers 4, 15, 18, 19, 21, 23, 26, 28, 31.)

Churches are made up of *people who are related in many different ways*. Family ties, professional connections, work friends, neighbors, and members of service clubs, all come together in the organism we call "church." It is common for people to be connected in more than one way. These different roles can cause confusion, and lead to conflict.

Think about this situation. The church council (or board) needs to decide whether to repair or replace the organ. The organist believes it needs to be replaced. The chair of the trustees is convinced that the organ everyone remembers can be restored for a trifling sum in comparison to the costs of replacement. The organist is the sister of the church council chairperson. The chair of the trustees is the employer of the church council chairperson. This sort of interrelationship and role confusion runs throughout the church.

Not only do we have role confusion because of the different ways we interconnect, we also have *different senses of our own boundaries*. Some people make decisions without thinking or caring what others may feel or think. Other people feel that approval of others is very important. They are paralyzed when needing to make a decision that will certainly make some people unhappy no matter what course is followed.

The sense of oneself as an individual interacting with other individuals can be described generally by the term "personal boundary dilemma." We generally know where the "self" ends and the next person begins.

A person with strong boundaries will feel that personal decisions, while needing to be made with reference to how others think and feel, are still personal. Persons with strong personal boundaries will be willing to risk disapproval, so long as they believe themselves to be right. This is different from being pigheaded or stubborn. Persons with strong personal boundaries will see themselves as autonomous actors, interacting with other autonomous actors.

Persons with weak or undefined personal boundaries tend to define themselves by how others define them. For example, if someone says they are clever, they believe they are clever. If someone says they sing well, they believe they sing well. Persons with weak personal boundaries get their approval from others, not from their inner sense of order, peace, and personal acceptance. They do not see themselves as autonomous individuals, but as part of a whole group. They identify with the group to such an extent that they do not have an independent personal identity.

For mature Christians, this inner sense of order, peace, and personal acceptance comes from how we believe God forgives and accepts us, and how we understand God calls us to live. Conformity to God's will is more important than conformity to the will of other individuals around us.

Most people are between these two extremes. Nearly everyone likes to receive the approval of others. The difference is in how important it is to their emotional and spiritual health. If we become depressed, or even ill because others criticize us, we have weak personal boundaries. If we become enraged because others disagree with us, our personal boundaries may be too strong. Neither of these extremes is healthy.

Boundaries violations occur in many different ways:

1. There is always someone in a church meeting with *strong opinions* who says what she or he thinks without seeming to care how it affects other people. There normally is also someone present who tries as hard as possible to *accommodate everyone* and offend no one. It is important to understand this range of personality difference and not allow the church to be dominated by only one style of self-definition and decision making.

2. Some people view all decision making in terms of a *power struggle and victimization*. Whenever a true power struggle occurs there truly are victims. But another way to work at this issue is to ensure that everyone in the group is invited to speak, and is given an equal ear. Then all the ideas may be placed on the table and evaluated for their merits. This helps to level differences in power, and returns the focus to problem-solving rather than seeing who can win.

3. A related issue is the *majority vote*. When decisions have to be made by a decision-rule (i.e., simple

majority, two-thirds, three-fourths, etc.) without giving careful attention to the valid concerns of the minority, disempowerment and weakness sets in. If all the concerns can be heard, and the whole group can work together toward genuine consensus, all individual boundaries are more adequately preserved.

4. Sometimes people utilize stories and arguments pertaining to *unrelated issues or conflicts* (sometimes even past conflicts). This only clouds the issue, and makes it more difficult to solve the specific problem that is currently on the table. The rule should always be, "Only one item on the table for discussion at a time. No other issues are allowed in."

5. Another boundary issue is utilizing *differences of interpretation* to serve as ammunition for seeking to win an argument. This can include doctrinal differences, differences in ethical positions, confusion over terminology, or disagreement over goals definition. The rule should be that when such confusion sets in everyone should return to common ground and start over. Once differences of interpretation are allowed to escalate no unity or problem-solving can occur.

6. Closely related to this is the tension over *freedom and spontaneity* in a church. Some people believe that everyone has to do the same thing at the same time in the same way. Others experience this as enslaving. While every congregation has the right to set their outer limits, allowing some flexibility and freedom of individual choice can be seen as spiritual grace.

7. Some churches have difficulty making decisions and then carrying them out. If the process is healthy and everyone has an opportunity for input, *coming to closure* is an essential component for staying healthy and moving on. A church that refuses to make and implement a decision because someone might be hurt really does a disservice and simply reinforces poor boundary definitions.

8. No discussion of boundary issues would be complete without mentioning a variety of *people abuses*. These range from sexual abuse and power abuse at one extreme to basic issues of sensitivity at the other. People have the right to their own private space and to an appropriate sense of dignity as persons. The church, of all places, has an obligation to support sexual integrity, the integrity of power, and the integrity of individuals as persons.[5]

No decision will satisfy everyone completely.

A church that demands that everyone be happy with every decision has weak personal boundaries. It says, "We are all one" in an unhealthy way. Where no dissent is tolerated, dissenters are forced either into hypocrisy or into leaving. Neither is it a healthy thing for a church to be dominated by a few strong personalities who say in effect, take it or leave it.

Good church decisions are worked at until they are acceptable to the whole group, and everyone agrees not to undercut or otherwise subvert the agreed upon decision. This means that everyone feels good about being heard, and either agrees with or consents to the decision that is made.

A church that can decide what to do in a way that has the support, if not the agreement of all members, has good boundaries. Individual members are not forced into a mold, but are invited into a cooperative relationship where different preferences rule at different times. Everyone is involved, and heard, when decisions need to be made.

God has a plan for us, but God also gave us free will. God did not see fit to turn us into puppets, blindly jerking to the pull of any master's strings. Neither did God intend the church to be a place where some members are the puppeteers and others are the puppets. The church is made up of autonomous individuals who have come together in obedience to God's will. Good decision-making processes will honor this commitment, and allow the church to work through controversy in a way that neither excludes nor enslaves.

It is good for our crises to be opportunities for transforming conflict into stronger and healthier relationships. That way the church and its individual members can truly be what God intended us to be. We can honor the individuality of each person while coming together in a group which is able to hear and respect each member. Doing that, we bring forth a synthesis of opinion that honors God and leads the church forward.

TO THINK ABOUT:

Which of the following cause difficulties in boundary-setting for your congregation?

❏ People with strong opinions—or those who try to accommodate everyone
❏ Issues of power and victimization
❏ The majority rules and the minority is not heard
❏ People who introduce old conflicts or unrelated topics into the decision-making process
❏ People with strong differences of interpretation
❏ Tension between freedom and spontaneity, conformity and diversity
❏ Difficulty in coming to closure on any decision and moving on
❏ People abuse issues
❏ Other _____

Which is the most problematic? What steps can you take right now to deal with the issues that cause boundary-setting problems in your congregation?

Chapter Four:

What Congregations Can Do to Help Themselves Resolve Conflict

We'll assume that some readers have completed the Congregational Conflict Type Indicator (CCTI, pages 9-12) and read chapters 1 through 3 already, while others have completed the CCTI and flipped over to this chapter. Still others have flipped quickly to this chapter in panic, to see what they can do quickly to deal with an immediate conflict.

One basic assumption you can make is that congregations who deal poorly with disagreements and conflict will also have difficulty dealing appropriately with a plan to resolve them. If that is true, how can you begin a conflict transformation process, and feel sure that you are following an appropriate plan? Following are some suggestions for beginning that process, regardless of the level of conflict you may be experiencing.

Beginning Steps

1. Invite a mutually acceptable person, with expertise in group process, to sit in and observe as you discuss your initial steps and process options. This individual should have some background and training in communication skills, group dynamics, and conflict transformation procedures. He or she should have the freedom to do some initial teaching and coach you through a healthy group planning process. District or conference-level church offices or other church leaders in your conference or region may be able to help identify such a person.

2. As you design a plan to transform the conflict in your group, *make sure everyone is clear on the goals of the plan*. If you decide on group meetings, are they for the purpose of simply clearing the air? Do you specifically want to clarify issues? Is your primary goal to hear different perspectives? Will it be necessary to make a decision of some sort? Do you have a major conflict to resolve?

3. Be sure to incorporate healthy group facilitation throughout the process. One resource on group facilitation provides this good overview of eight basic principles: [1]
   • Be clear on your procedures before beginning.
   • Be participatory; make sure all individuals affected by the decision are involved in the discussion and decision-making process.
   • Develop multiple options before beginning the decision-making process.
   • Allow the expression of different points of view at all times.
   • Provide adequate time and structures so everyone can be heard.
   • Allow input to come in a variety of ways (large groups, small groups, individual interviews, paper surveys, etc.).
   • Keep information open, clear, and complete. Make sure data gathered from the group about the group is adequately reported back.
   • Make sure there are no surprises. Keep people well informed in advance, and take straw polls as needed so everyone can respond appropriately before a final vote is taken.

4. It is also good to *keep your initial goals concise and simple* (and to work on only one goal at a time). Do not fall into the trap of trying to accomplish several goals in one quick meeting. That may be possible when you are dealing with a non-controversial topic, but it seldom works well when groups are dealing with conflict.

5. Another step you can take is to clearly *identify the types and levels of conflict* that may be present in the congregation. Perhaps your leadership group has already completed the CCTI. If you have, you may make additional copies of the instrument and invite members of the congregation to complete it also.

A simple tool to help identify the levels of conflict present in your group is the "Levels of Conflict" Indicator, found in Appendix A (pages 51-52). (Refer to chapter 2 to determine appropriate responses at these different levels of conflict.) As you evaluate the type/s of conflict present in the congregation, and the levels at which they operate, you can make better decisions about what steps to take next.

6. An additional step might be to *study the available literature* listed in Appendix C (pages 55-57). Much of that material includes healthy steps for conflict transformation and the healthy development of congregational systems.

As part of your study, you may also wish to secure conflict transformation training for your church board and/or congregation. Some of the organizations listed in Appendix D (page 58) offer training programs and would be glad to assist you.

Steps for Specific Types of Conflicts

Some basic, simple steps for addressing conflict surrounding the five types of conflicts identified in chapter 3 include the following.

For conflicts involving a breakdown in *interpersonal relationships*, try the following:

Seek once more to initiate direct dialogue with others in the conflict, only this time do not spend your time telling them "what the answer is." Instead, follow the counsel of Philippians 2:4, "each of you look not to your own interests, but to the interests of others." Invite them to present their views, and also listen to your views. Don't try to change each other, but to understand each other better. Then identify the common issue, or the interest you both have, and seek a solution that satisfies everyone.

If that fails, invite the other side to enter into a process of mediation with you. You may secure counsel from your conference minister, bishop, or overseer in selecting a mediator, or you may each name two mediators, and then select the one that comes closest to meeting the expectations of everyone.

For conflicts involving poor *communication* try the following:

Evaluate the way in which you inform people in the church about congregational issues. Take several steps to improve information sharing.

Provide, very openly, for ways the congregation can give good feedback on issues pertaining to them. Make it clear that not every suggestion will be followed, but that all ideas will be received with appreciation. Then, later on, communicate about ways in which their feedback helped you give better leadership.

For conflicts involving poor *decision-making styles*, try the following:

Evaluate your decision-making policy in general, and your specific decision-making approach as it pertains to the situation involved in the conflict. If you find weaknesses or gaps in a good decision-making process, address the process before proceeding with the decision.

You may also want to do some research into good decision-making styles, and allow congregational input into what they believe is a good decision-making style for your church. Use that combined information to strengthen your congregational decision-making style.

For conflicts involving *leadership issues*, try the following:

Talk about the ways pastoral leadership, lay leadership, and unofficial leaders in the church can work together as a team to keep the church united and focused at the problem-solving level of all conflicts.

Discuss ways in which the whole leadership team can keep the congregation better informed, and draw them into the decision-making process in a healthier way.

Evaluate different approaches to conflict transformation in the congregation, and determine which lay leaders should best carry that responsibility.

For conflicts involving *boundary issues*, try the following:

Talk about the importance of respecting the views of everyone in the church, even when they are different from the views of others. Talk about how that can happen without labeling one as wrong and the other as right. Find ways to implement the spirit of Philippians 2:4.

Talk about how you can accept those who disagree with you without taking it personally. Realize that seeing things differently doesn't mean that you are rejected as a person. Study the way Jesus accepted all of his disciples even though they were of many different temperaments and had strongly diverse viewpoints on many issues. [2]

Agree that all of you will support the decisions made by the congregation even though it may not have been your personal choice. Talk about ways you can put Philippians 2:2 ("make my joy complete: be of the same mind, having the same love, being in full accord and of one mind") into practice in seeking the integrity of the unity of the body of Christ.

Conflict Transformation Basic Plan

Finally, here's a simple, basic plan that can help you resolve some conflicts in your congregation before they tear you apart.

- Clearly identify the issue or issues.
- Commit yourselves to work together to find a solution that addresses the issue, not the personalities involved.
- Commit yourselves to honor God and one another.
- Develop a plan of action so the solution you agree to can be accomplished.

When No Serious Conflict Is Present

What if there is currently no intense, divisive, destructive conflict in your congregation? Is there anything you can do to prevent it from happening in the future?

Yes, there is. The most important thing you can do is to establish healthy norms for congregational life. Talk together, do some research, check with conference or regional leadership, check with a consultant, and develop appropriate normative ways in which you want your congregational life to function. The areas of concern could include:

- Appropriate behaviors for interpersonal relationships
- Acceptable communication standards and styles
- Adequate decision-making procedures
- Reliable leadership standards
- Responsible boundaries definitions.

In addition, it is also helpful to have an adequate conflict resolution policy in place, so that whenever anyone in the congregation experiences a personal or organizational conflict, he or she can have confidence that by following the accepted policy the conflict has a better chance of being resolved satisfactorily.

One such agreement is the document "Agreeing and Disagreeing in Love," developed by the Peace and Justice Commission of the Mennonite Church. An abbreviated form of the text follows.[3]

Agreeing and Disagreeing in Love

"Making every effort to maintain the unity of the Spirit in the bond of peace" (Eph. 4:3), as both individual members and the body of Christ, we pledge that we shall:

1. *Accept conflict.* Acknowledge together that conflict is a normal part of our life in the church.
   Romans 14:1-8, 10-12, 17-19; 15:1-7
2. *Affirm hope.* Affirm that as God walks with us in conflict we can work through to growth.
   Ephesians 4:15-16
3. *Commit to prayer.* Admit our needs and commit ourselves to pray for a mutually satisfactory solution (no prayers for my success or for the other to change but to find a joint way).
   James 5:16
4. *Go to the other . . .* Go directly to those with whom we disagree; avoid behind-the-back criticism. (Go directly if you are European-North American. In other cultures disagreements are often addressed through a trusted go-between.)
   Matthew 5:23-24; 18:15-20
5. *. . . in the spirit of humility.* Go in gentleness, patience, and humility. Place the problem between us at neither doorstep and own our part in the conflict instead of pointing out the others.
   Galatians 6:1-5
6. *Be quick to listen.* Listen carefully, summarize and check out what is heard before responding. Seek as much to understand as to be understood.
   James 1:19; Proverbs 18:13

7. *Be slow to judge.* Suspend judgments, avoid labeling, end name calling, discard threats, and act in a nondefensive, nonreactive way.
   Romans 2:1-4; Galatians 5:22-26

8. *Be willing to negotiate.* Work through the disagreements constructively.
   Acts 15; Philippians 2:1-11
   - Identify issues, interests, and needs of both (rather than take positions).
   - Generate a variety of options for meeting both parties' needs (rather than defending one's own way).
   - Evaluate options by how they meet the needs and satisfy the interests of all sides (not one side's values).
   - Collaborate in working out a joint solution (so both sides gain, both grow and win).
   - Cooperate with the emerging agreement (accept the possible, not demand your ideal).
   - Reward each other for each step forward, toward agreement (celebrate mutuality).

9. *Be steadfast in love.* Be firm in our commitment to seek a mutual solution; be stubborn in holding to our common foundation in Christ; be steadfast in love.
   Colossians 3:12-15

10. *Be open to mediation.* Be open to accept skilled help. If we cannot reach agreement among ourselves, we will use those with gifts and training in mediation in the larger church.
    Philippians 4:1-3

11. *Trust the community.* We will trust the community and if we cannot reach agreement or experience reconciliation, we will turn the decision over to others in the congregation or from the broader church.
    Acts 15.
    - In one-to-one or small-group disputes, this may mean allowing others to arbitrate.
    - In congregational, conference district, or denominational disputes, this may mean allowing others to arbitrate or implementing constitutional decision-making processes, insuring that they are done in the spirit of these guidelines, and abiding by whatever decision is made.

12. *Be the body of Christ.* Believe in and rely on the solidarity of the body of Christ and its commitment to peace and justice, rather than resort to the courts of law.
    1 Corinthians 6:1-6

(Adopted by the General Conference Mennonite Church Triennial Session and Mennonite Church General Assembly, Wichita, Kan., July 1995.)

Pontius' Puddle

Chapter Five:

Getting Help from Outside Resources

Let's assume you've worked through the Congregational Conflict Type Indicator (CCTI) and the first four chapters of this manual. You've done all you can yourself and feel you need help from outside resources. How do you begin?

Working closely with the official leadership group of your congregation and appropriate denominational resources, determine as closely as you can your goals and the type of assistance you feel you need to help you accomplish those goals. Listed below are ten examples of goals you may be seeking:

- Experience congregational healing in the wake of a painful conflict.
- Deal with long-standing congregational issues which get in the way of healthy church growth and prevent effective ministry.
- Avoid a split in the church.
- Retain a pastor who's threatening to resign.
- Confront issues of abuse of power (or sexual abuse, or financial mismanagement, etc.).
- Mediate between two or more views of an issue facing the church.
- Learn how to be more effective in congregational communication styles.
- Assess leadership style issues.
- Design a specific conflict transformation policy for the church.
- Other _____

What type of assistance do you believe may be beneficial?

❏ A consultation from a specialist in church systems or organizational dynamics.
❏ An intervention from an outside mediator or conflict resolution specialist.
❏ Facilitated dialogue between groups of people in the congregation.
❏ A training program designed to assist the congregation in increasing skills or accomplishing certain objectives.
❏ Other _____

Once you have identified the specific areas of concern that you are facing, ask your denominational office (conference minister, bishop, or overseer, etc.) for a list of recommended agencies and individuals who may assist you. Or, contact the networking agencies listed in Appendix D (page 58).

Identify a trusted spokesperson in the church who can make the outside contacts for you, in a timely, clear, and impartial manner. This person should also be empowered to negotiate on your behalf, with the understanding that no final decisions will be made without clear guidance from the authorized leadership body of the congregation.

When you contact organizations and/or individual consultants or mediators for assistance, be specific in your request. Remain open, however, to the assessment role and process suggestions of the specialists you are contacting. The trusted spokesperson from the congregation will:

- Identify the type and level of conflict or other issue you may be confronting. (Avoid the desire to offer a long narrative of your view of the problem/s. Give only a brief specific overview of the issue/s, following the recommendations of your leadership group. State the outcome you desire as the result of obtaining outside assistance.)
- Identify the type of training you are looking for, and also the outcome you desire as a result of the training.
- Identify any other specific assistance you may desire, and the objective you have in view for that assistance.
- Indicate your willingness to allow the specialist you select to suggest revisions in your assessment of the issues and approach to seeking the solutions you desire. Remember that the

right assessment and plan design, drawn up during the early stages of assistance, may be invaluable in moving toward adequate solutions. (Some consultants actually contract for an assessment phase, after which further plans are negotiated.)

To help in your selection process of outside assistance, the trusted spokesperson will seek the following information from each professional contact:

- What is their philosophy and approach to providing services?
- What is the training and background of the individual/s who would provide the service?
- What is their availability?
- What costs can you anticipate?
- What references can they provide?

After this information has been secured from two or more contacts, report back the information to the church governing body responsible for making the final choice. If it is practical, arrange for a face-to-face interview between the proposed consultant/s and key leaders of the church. Provide adequate information about the selection process to the congregation, and allow for appropriate input, so the congregation may experience full buy-in of the proposed intervention.

Be clear from the outset about who has the authority to make the final selection of the outside helper. This also pertains to who has the authority to negotiate and approve the actual contract and the process plan to be implemented. Also determine who will be the contact person/s once the consultant, mediator, or trainer is engaged. (Sometimes the outside individual or team will want to offer input into establishing these internal contacts, including the possibility of a representative reference group to help with assessment and ongoing communication tasks within the congregation.)

Also be sure to clarify the role and communication lines for district, conference, or regional-level leadership, as appropriate for your polity and the intervention process that is chosen. Whatever lines of communication are established, both internally and externally, take steps to ensure that they remain clear and open, and that appropriate boundaries are always respected.

A final step which can be very helpful in preparing for outside assistance is to record a congregational vote or consensus statement ratifying the action of the governing body and showing a definite commitment to accepting the help that will be offered. This is important even if your polity does not require a congregational vote. Having a vote ensures stronger congregational buy-in.

Don't forget to spend time in prayer as a congregation, a leadership team, and as individuals, asking God to bless the efforts that will be put forth.

Once these steps are completed, contact the agency, team, or individual you have chosen and negotiate the final terms of the agreement.

"Levels of Conflict" Evaluator (see chapter 2).

Prepared by Marlin E. Thomas

Instructions: This evaluator combines the insights of chapters 2 and 3. Score the following sets of items on a scale of 0 to 10, to gauge the level of conflict (chapter 2) that you feel may currently exist in your congregation in each of the five arenas of systems failure (chapter 3). The item in each arena of systems failure with the highest score may indicate the *level* of conflict (from 1 to 5) your congregation is experiencing in each arena. Review chapter 2 to determine appropriate ways of dealing with each level of conflict, and review chapter 3 to determine appropriate ways of dealing with each arena of a systems failure. (For example, if your highest score in Arena 1 is a 5 on question 2, your highest score in Arena 2 is a 9 on question 5, your highest score in Arena 3 is a 7 on question 1, etc., that may indicate that the congregation is experiencing a significant Level Two conflict in Arena 1, a very intense Level Five conflict in Arena 2, and a significant Level 1 conflict in Arena 3. You should get outside help immediately to address the issues in Arenas 3 and 2, and consider getting outside help with Arena 1. If your scores are all at or below three, you may be able to work at the conflicts yourselves.)

Conflict Arena One: Interpersonal Relationships
Individuals in our congregation who currently disagree over an issue:
1. *are talking things out with each other so the conflict can be resolved justly.*
   Never True   0   1   2   3   4   5   6   7   8   9   10   Always True
2. *are talking mainly to their friends about the problem.*
   Never True   0   1   2   3   4   5   6   7   8   9   10   Always True
3. *have chosen sides and sometimes seek additional supporters from within the congregation.*
   Never True   0   1   2   3   4   5   6   7   8   9   10   Always True
4. *warn of "serious consequences" to follow if things don't change.*
   Never True   0   1   2   3   4   5   6   7   8   9   10   Always True
5. *threaten others if they refuse to change, but themselves refuse to change.*
   Never True   0   1   2   3   4   5   6   7   8   9   10   Always True

Conflict Arena Two: Communication/Information Sharing
Individuals in our congregation who currently disagree over an issue:
1. *are sharing information with each other openly and honestly.*
   Never True   0   1   2   3   4   5   6   7   8   9   10   Always True
2. *are only sharing partial information in a vague and unclear manner.*
   Never True   0   1   2   3   4   5   6   7   8   9   10   Always True
3. *are subjective and one-sided in talking about the issues.*
   Never True   0   1   2   3   4   5   6   7   8   9   10   Always True
4. *talk about the "right side" and the "wrong side" in the conflict.*
   Never True   0   1   2   3   4   5   6   7   8   9   10   Always True
5. *talk about the issue(s) in terms of good and evil, with their opponents being seen as agents of evil, needing to be expelled or forced to change for the spiritual good of the church.*
   Never True   0   1   2   3   4   5   6   7   8   9   10   Always True

Conflict Arena Three: Managing Emotions

Individuals in our congregation who currently disagree over an issue:

1. *own their own feelings about the disagreement and report them to others in the dispute, mutually caring for each other emotionally and spiritually.*

Never True   0   1   2   3   4   5   6   7   8   9   10   Always True

2. *are touchy and guarded, yet sometimes deny that anything is wrong.*

Never True   0   1   2   3   4   5   6   7   8   9   10   Always True

3. *are emotionally tense and anxious, justifying their feelings on the basis of the misdeeds of others.*

Never True   0   1   2   3   4   5   6   7   8   9   10   Always True

4. *are so emotionally traumatized that sometimes their personality and behavior seems to change.*

Never True   0   1   2   3   4   5   6   7   8   9   10   Always True

5. *are so emotionally hardened that the atmosphere feels like ice.*

Never True   0   1   2   3   4   5   6   7   8   9   10   Always True

Conflict Arena Four: Accepting the Views of Others

Individuals in our congregation who currently disagree over an issue:

1. *respect other persons' views, even if they don't agree with them.*

Never True   0   1   2   3   4   5   6   7   8   9   10   Always True

2. *don't take other people's views seriously if they're different.*

Never True   0   1   2   3   4   5   6   7   8   9   10   Always True

3. *reject the views of others with whom they disagree.*

Never True   0   1   2   3   4   5   6   7   8   9   10   Always True

4. *describe other views, with which they disagree, as being sinful, unbiblical, or un-Christlike.*

Never True   0   1   2   3   4   5   6   7   8   9   10   Always True

5. *are on a crusade to discredit and destroy the views with which they disagree.*

Never True   0   1   2   3   4   5   6   7   8   9   10   Always True

Conflict Arena Five: Dealing with Differences

Individuals in our congregation who currently disagree over an issue:

1. *negotiate their differences in a way that everyone can be satisfied with the outcome.*

Never True   0   1   2   3   4   5   6   7   8   9   10   Always True

2. *debate their differences with each other without yielding any ground.*

Never True   0   1   2   3   4   5   6   7   8   9   10   Always True

3. *distort and magnify the differences which exist in the conflict.*

Never True   0   1   2   3   4   5   6   7   8   9   10   Always True

4. *see the differences as being clearly divided with no middle ground in between.*

Never True   0   1   2   3   4   5   6   7   8   9   10   Always True

5. *seem to be in the midst of a crusade to set everyone else straight and get everyone back on the right track again.*

Never True   0   1   2   3   4   5   6   7   8   9   10   Always True

Interpretation: By way of review, chapter 2 identifies a Level One conflict as one in which the group deals with conflict as problems to solve, a Level Two conflict as one in which there is discomfort and definite disagreement, a Level Three conflict as one in which two or more sides are in a contest which each side feels they must win, a Level Four conflict as the fight or flee stage of conflict, and a Level Five conflict as intractable—one in which no one is willing any longer to seek a mutually workable solution, and everyone loses. Chapter 2 also indicates that local congregations usually cannot successfully resolve Level Three or higher conflicts by themselves. They need outside help. Therefore, if the highest scores in each arena of failure are in items 3, 4, or 5, you need to seek outside help. The higher the numbers scored on each item (from 0 to 10), the more significant that conflict is, and the more quickly you need to take positive action to address the situation.

Appendix B:
Conflict Management Styles Instruments

Conflict Management Survey, by Jay Hall
    Teleometrics International
    1755 Woodstead Court
    The Woodlands, TX 77380-0964
    Phone: 281-367-0060; 800-527-0406

Designed to provide you with information about your approach to managing conflict. It will help individuals understand more about themselves and their behaviors in conflict situations. It is divided into four major categories appropriate to conflict issues (personal orientation to conflict, interpersonal conflict, conflict within a group, conflict between groups). Developed primarily for the business world.

Conflict Styles Survey, by Norman Shawchuck
    Spiritual Growth Resources
    Cottontail Ridge
    7909 64th Ave. SW
    Leith, ND 58529
    Phone: 1-800-359-7363

Composed of a series of twelve situations often encountered in church leadership, this survey is designed to assist the individual in assessing and developing an understanding of his or her behavior in conflict situations. It uses the five conflict management styles discussed here in chapter 1, Collaborating, Compromising, Accommodating, Avoiding, and Forcing.

Discover Your Conflict Management Style, rev. ed., by Speed Leas
    The Alban Institute
    7315 Wisconsin Avenue, Suite 1250 West
    Bethesda, MD 20814-3211
    Phone: 1-800-486-1318

Helps you self-assess your conflict response (persuasive, compelling, avoiding, accommodating, collaborating, negotiating, and supportive) and discover options appropriate to different levels of conflict. Was developed specifically with church conflict situations in mind.

Style Profile for Communication at Work, by Susan Gilmore and Patrick Fraleigh
    Friendly Press
    2744 Friendly Street
    Eugene, OR 97405
    Phone: 541-741-8864
    Fax: 541-988-1002

An inventory of twenty items, this is designed to help the individual better understand him or herself at work. It assesses reactions under calm and storm conditions, using the four traits of Accommodating/Harmonizing, Analyzing/Preserving, Achieving/Directing, and Affiliating/Perfecting.

Thomas-Kilmann Conflict Mode Instrument, by Kenneth W. Thomas and Ralph H. Kilmann
    Consulting Psychologists Press
    3803 E. Bayshore Road
    Palo Alto, CA 94303
    Phone: 1-800-624-1765

Designed to assess an individual's behavior in conflict situations. It is a self-directed exercise using forced-choice responses in theoretical conflict situations. It shows how people typically manage conflict (collaborating, compromising, accommodating, avoiding, competing), explaining how different conflict situations require the flexible use of one or more strategic intentions. Developed primarily for the business world.

What Is Your Conflict Management Style, by Ron Kraybill
> Mennonite Conciliation Service
> 21 S. 12th St., P.O. Box 500
> Akron, PA 17501
> Phone: 717-859-3889

This instrument is available in *Mediation and Facilitation Training Manual,* 4th ed., Carolyn Shrock-Shenk, ed.

Appendix C:
Literature and Resources

Attitude and Process in Conflict Resolution

Augsburger, David. *Caring Enough to Forgive/Caring Enough Not to Forgive*. Scottdale: Herald Press, 1982.
____. *Helping People Forgive*. Louisville, Ky.: Westminster John Knox Press, 1996.
Fisher, Roger and Scott Brown. *Getting Together: Building Relationships as We Negotiate*. New York: Penguin Books, 1988.
Fisher, Roger and William Ury. *Getting to Yes: Negotiating Agreement Without Giving In*. New York: Penguin Books, 1981.
Friedmann, J. M. *Helping Resolve Conflict*. Scottdale: Herald Press, 1990.
Kliewer, Stephen. *How to Live with Diversity in the Local Church*. Bethesda, Md.: The Alban Institute, 1990.
McCollough, Charles R. *Resolving Conflict with Justice and Peace*. New York: Pilgrim Press, 1991.
Prinzing, Fred. *Handling Church Tensions Creatively: Adjusting Twelve Tensions to Avoid Conflict*. Arlington Heights, Ill.: Harvest Publishers, 1986.
Qualben, James. *Peace in the Parish: How to Use Conflict Redemption Principles and Process*. San Antonio: Langmarc Publishing, 1991.
Schrock-Shenk, Carolyn and Lawrence Ressler, eds. *Making Peace with Conflict: Practical Skills for Conflict Transformation*. Scottdale: Herald Press, 1999.
Ury, William. *Getting Past No: Negotiating Your Way from Confrontation to Cooperation*. New York: Bantam Books, 1991.
Washburn, Patricia and Robert Gribbon. *Peacemaking Without Division: Moving Beyond Congregational Apathy and Anger*. Bethesda, Md.: The Alban Institute, 1986.
Willimon, William. *Preaching About Conflict in the Local Church*. Philadelphia: Westminster Press, 1987.

Communication

Augsburger, David. *Caring Enough to Confront: How to Understand and Express Your Deepest Feelings Toward Others*. Scottdale: Herald Press, 1973.
____. *Caring Enough to Hear and Be Heard*. Scottdale: Herald Press, 1982.
____. *When Caring Is Not Enough: Resolving Conflicts through Fair Fighting*. Scottdale: Herald Press, 1983.
Bartel, Barry. *Let's Talk: Communication Skills and Conflict Transformation*. Newton, Kan.: Faith & Life Press, 1999.
Cloud, Henry and John Townsend. *Boundaries: When to Say Yes, When to Say No, to Take Control of Your Life*. Grand Rapids, Mich.: Zondervan, 1992.
Fairfield, James. *When You Don't Agree*. Scottdale: Herald Press, 1977.
Koch, Ruth and Kenneth C. Haugk. *Speaking the Truth in Love: How to Be an Assertive Christian*. St. Louis: Stephen Ministries, 1992.
Morris, Danny E. and Charles M. Olsen. *Discerning God's Will Together*. Bethesda, Md.: The Alban Institute, 1997.
Swets, Paul W. *The Art of Talking So That People Will Listen: Getting Through to Family, Friends and Business Associates*. New York: Simon and Schuster, 1983.
Vincent, Mark. *Art of Agreement: Good Committee Process for God's People*. Sturgis Press, 1995.

Healing

Cook, Jerry. *Love, Acceptance and Forgiveness*. Ventura, Calif.: Regal Books, 1979.

Edwards, Gene. *Letters to a Devastated Christian*. Auburn, Maine: Christian Books, 1984.

Jones, L. Gregory. *Embodying Forgiveness: A Theological Analysis*. Grand Rapids, Mich.: Eerdmans, 1995.

White, John and Ken Blue. *Healing the Wounded*. Downers Grove, Ill: InterVarsity Press, 1985.

Intercultural / Interracial

Augsburger, David. *Conflict Mediation Across Cultures: Pathways and Patterns*. Louisville, Ky.: Westminster/John Knox, 1992.

Lederach, John Paul. *Preparing for Peace: Conflict Transformation Across Cultures*. Syracuse, N.Y.: Syracuse University, 1995.

Ruth-Heffelbower, Duane. *Conflict and Peacemaking Across Cultures: Training for Trainers*. Fresno, Calif.: Fresno Pacific University, 1999.

Washington, Raleigh and Glen Kehrein. *Breaking Down Walls: A Model for Reconciliation in an Age of Racial Strife*. Chicago: Moody Press, 1993.

Intervention / Consultation

Leas, Speed. *Moving Your Church Through Conflict*. Bethesda, Md.: The Alban Institute, 1985.

Shrock-Shenk, Carolyn, ed. *Mediation and Facilitation Training Manual*. 4th ed. Akron, Pa.: Mennonite Conciliation Service, 2000.

Walton, Richard E. *Interpersonal Peacemaking: Confrontations and Third-Party Consultation*. Reading, Mass.: Addison-Wesley Publishing Co., 1969.

Introduction to Conflict Resolution / General Works

Boers, Arthur Paul. *Never Call Them Jerks: Healthy Responses to Difficult Behavior*. Bethesda, Md.: Alban Institute, 1999.

Dobson, James, Speed Leas, and Marshall Shelley. *Mastering Conflict and Controversy*. Portland, Ore.: Multnomah Press and Christianity Today, 1992.

Halverstadt, Hugh. *Managing Church Conflict*. Louisville, Ky.: Westminster/John Knox Press, 1991.

Hocker, Joyce L. and William W. Wilmot. *Interpersonal Conflict*. 4th ed. Dubuque, Iowa: Wm. C. Brown, Publishers, 1974, 1995.

Huttenlocker, Keith. *Conflict and Caring: Preventing, Managing and Resolving Conflict in the Church*. Grand Rapids, Mich.: Zondervan, 1988.

Krieder, Robert S. and Rachel Waltner Goossen. *When Good People Quarrel: Studies in Conflict Resolution*. Scottdale: Herald Press, 1989.

Leas, Speed. *A Lay Person's Guide to Conflict Management*. Bethesda, Md.: The Alban Institute, 1979.

____. *Leadership and Conflict*. Nashville: Abingdon Press, 1982.

____. and Paul Kittlaus. *Church Fights: Managing Conflict in the Local Church*. Philadelphia: Westminster Press, 1973.

Lederach, John Paul. *The Journey Toward Reconciliation*. Scottdale: Herald Press, 1999.

Peters, Dave. *Surviving Church Conflict*. Scottdale: Herald Press, 1997.

Roberts, Wes. *Support Your Local Pastor: Practical Ways to Encourage Your Minister*. Colorado Springs: NavPress, 1995.

Saarinen, Martin F. *The Life Cycle of a Congregation*. Bethesda, Md.: The Alban Institute, 1986.

Sande, Ken. *The Peacemaker: A Biblical Guide to Resolving Personal Conflict*. Grand Rapids, Mich.: Baker Book House, 1991.

Shawchuck, Norman. *How to Manage Conflict in the Church: Understanding and Managing Conflict*. 2 vols. Leith, N.D.: Spiritual Growth Resources, 1983.

Shelley, Marshall, gen. ed. *Leading Your Church Through Conflict and Reconciliation*. Minneapolis: Bethany House Publishers, 1997.

Thomas, Marlin. *Resolving Disputes in Christian Groups*. Winnipeg, Mass.: Windflower Communications, 1994.

_____. *Solving Disagreements in the Church: A Biblical Base*. Rev. ed. Lancaster, Pa.: Resources for Resolving Conflict, 1993.

Voges, Ken and Ron Braund. *Understanding How Others Misunderstand You*. Chicago: Moody Press, 1990.

Wecks, John. *Free to Disagree: Moving Beyond the Arguments Over Christian Liberty*. Grand Rapids, Mich.: Kregel Publications, 1996.

White, James E. and Robert L. Sheffield. *Equipping Deacons to Confront Conflict*. Nashville: Convention Press, 1987.

Sexual Boundaries

Fortune, Marie Marshall. *Sexual Violence, The Unmentionable Sin: An Ethical and Pastoral Perspective*. Cleveland, Ohio: Pilgrim Press, 1983.

Hayford, Jack W. *Restoring Fallen Leaders*. Ventura, Calif.: Regal Books, 1988.

Heggen, Carolyn Holderread. *Sexual Abuse in Christian Homes and Churches*. Scottdale: Herald Press, 1993.

Hopkins, Nancy Myer and Mark Laaser, eds. *Restoring the Soul of a Church: Healing Congregations Wounded by Clergy Sexual Misconduct*. Bethesda, Md.: The Alban Institute, 1995.

LaHaye, Tim. *If Ministers Fall, Can They Be Restored?* Grand Rapids, Mich.: Zondervan, 1990.

Lebacqz, Karen and Ronald G. Barton. *Sex in the Parish*. Louisville, Ky.: Westminster/John Knox, 1991.

Pastoral Sexual Misconduct: A Resource Packet, Mennonite Board of Congregational Ministries, 1996. (Also available from Conference of Mennonites in Canada, Winnipeg, Man.).

Rutter, Peter. *Sex in the Forbidden Zone: When Men in Power—Therapists, Doctors, Clergy, Teachers, and Others—Betray Women's Trust*. New York: Fawcett Press, 1983.

Schaumburg, Harry W. *False Intimacy: Understanding the Struggle of Sexual Addiction*. Colorado Springs: NavPress, 1992.

Winebrenner, Jan and Debra Frazier. *When a Leader Falls, What Happens to Everyone Else?* Minneapolis: Bethany House, 1993.

Yantzi, Mark. *Sexual Offending and Restoration*. Waterloo, Ont.: Herald Press, 1998.

Systems Issues in Conflict Resolution

Cosgrove, Charles H. and Dennis D. Hatfield. *Church Conflict: The Hidden Systems Behind the Fights*. Nashville: Abingdon Press, 1994.

Edwards, Lloyd. *How We Belong, Fight, and Pray: The MBTI as a Key to Congregational Dynamics*. Bethesda, Md.: The Alban Institute, 1993.

Friedman, Edwin H. *Generation to Generation: Family Process in Church and Synagogue*. New York: Guilford Press, 1985.

Jeschke, Marlin. *Discipling in the Church*. Scottdale: Herald Press, 1988.

Mains, David. *Healing the Dysfunctional Church Family: When Destructive Family Patterns Infiltrate the Body of Christ*. Wheaton, Ill.: Victor Books, 1992.

Mitchell, Kenneth R. *Multiple Staff Ministries*. Louisville, Ky.: Westminster Press, 1988.

Richardson, Ronald W. *Creating a Healthier Church*. Minneapolis: Fortress Press, 1996.

Shawchuck, Norman. *How to Manage Conflict in the Church: Dysfunctional Congregations*. Leith, N.D.: Spiritual Growth Resources, 1996.

Steinke, Peter L. *Healthy Congregations: A Systems Approach*. Bethesda, Md.: The Alban Institute, 1997.

_____. *How Your Church Family Works: Understanding Congregations as Emotional Systems*. Bethesda, Md.: The Alban Institute, 1993.

Audio and Video

Conflict in the Church, 40 min. video cassette. Akron, Pa.: Mennonite Conciliation Service, 1999.

Conflict in the Church: Division or Diversity, 12 min. video cassette. Akron, Pa.: Mennonite Conciliation Service, 1988.

When You Disagree, 6-cassette audio series. Akron, Pa.: Mennonite Conciliation Service.

Church Conflict Solutions 101, 14-cassette audio series. Lancaster, Pa.: Resources for Resolving Conflict, 1999. Order by calling 717-393-9964, or e-mail info@rrcinc.org.

Appendix D:
Conflict Resolution Consultants and Mediation Networks

The Alban Institute
> John Janka, contact person
> Suite 1250 West
> 7315 Wisconsin Avenue
> Bethesda, MD 20814-3341
> Phone: 1-800-486-1318, ext. 229, fax: 301-718-1958
> E-mail: jjanka@alban.org

Leadership Journal
> See list of consultants and mediators, Spring 1998 issue, pages 65-66.
> Kevin A. Miller, editor
> 465 Gundersen Drive
> Carol Stream, IL 60188
> Phone: 630-260-6200, fax: 630-260-0114
> E-mail: LeaderJ@aol.com

Conciliation Services Canada
> Nan Cressman
> 258 Lakeshore Drive, R.R. 1
> Desbarats, ON Canada P0R 1E0
> Phone: 705-782-0287, fax: 705-782-6276
> E-mail: cressman@soonet.ca

Mennonite Conciliation Service
> Michelle Armster, contact person
> 21 S. 12th Street, P.O. Box 500
> Akron, PA 17501
> Phone: 717-859-3889, fax: 717-859-3875
> E-mail: mcs@mccus.org

Ministry of Reconciliation (Church of the Brethren)
> Bob Gross, contact person
> On Earth Peace
> P. O. Box 188
> New Windsor, MD 21776
> Phone/fax: 260-982-7751
> E-mail: bgross_oepa@brethren.org

Peacemaker Ministries (Institute for Christian Conciliation)
> David Edling, contact person
> 1537 Avenue D, Suite 352
> Billings, MT 59102
> Phone: 406-256-1583, fax: 406-256-0001
> E-mail: mail@HisPeace.org

Appendix E:
Historic Conflicts in the Church

Council of Nicea: This (first) council of bishops was called in A.D. 325 to settle a dispute over the deity of Christ. Arius, an elderly presbyter and popular preacher of Alexandria, Egypt, feared that the teaching of the Trinity would lead the people back into paganism (belief in multiple gods), so he taught that only God the Father had existed from eternity. Christ was then created by God the Father, who then called upon Christ to create all things according to God's perfect plan. Thus, Jesus was not coeternal with the Father. Athanasius, a younger presbyter in Alexandria, strongly defended the teaching that Jesus is coeternal and equal with the Father. This created a severe conflict for the entire church, which was addressed first at the Council of Nicea in 325, and finally settled fifty-six years later in Constantinople at the (second) council of bishops in A.D. 381.

Martin Luther's Ninety-Five Theses: During the Renaissance the church experienced many growing pains. Many of these had to do with the tension between earthly power and spirituality. During Martin Luther's early life as a monk, he lectured regularly on the Bible in the University of Wittenberg. At the same time, another monk, Tetzel, was hawking indulgences (monetary certificates of merit for the forgiveness of sin) to finance the building of St. Peter's Church in Rome. Martin Luther did not believe that indulgences were a biblically correct way to receive forgiveness of sin. He especially detested their use to finance expensive church building programs. He therefore wrote out ninety-five statements to prove his point, and tacked them to the door of the castle church in Wittenberg on October 31, 1517. They were published far and wide, and discussion about them began a revival that swept the Roman Catholic world.

In the severe church conflict that followed, Martin was summoned to Rome for correction. Because of his firm belief in justification through faith alone, and his refusal to accept correction from the bishops, he was excommunicated. He was then put on trial as a heretic in Germany, but rescued by his governor, Frederick the Wise. Thus, in an effort to reform the church and bring the gospel of justification through faith to his (German) people, the Protestant Reformation began.

Conrad Grebel's Dispute with the City Council over Baptism: The year after Martin Luther had tacked the ninety-five theses to the church door in Wittenberg, pastor Ulrich Zwingli in Zurich, Switzerland, also began preaching against indulgences. He also began reforming the church in Zurich in other ways, with support from the city council. During that time he met with a small group of young men for regular Tuesday evening Bible studies, including Conrad Grebel, Felix Manz, and George Blaurock. As they studied the gospels, they became convicted that theirs was an empty faith based more on works than on a dynamic faith in Jesus Christ. They began to see, among other things, that baptism should follow conversion. When they wanted to replace infant baptism with believer's baptism, Zwingli hesitated, because the city council refused to give their blessing. This caused the young men to withdraw from Zwingli.

On January 21, 1525, about twelve men gathered for an evening Bible study. During a time of prayer they confessed their sins and were then baptized upon the confession of their faith. During the next several months and years the new Anabaptist movement grew rapidly and experienced great persecution. Out of this severe conflict a new reformation movement was born, holding that believers are a community of the faithful, and must first be loyal to the kingdom of God. It was the beginning of the "free church" movement.

Vatican II: Beginning with the Council of Nicea in A.D. 325, the Western (Roman Catholic) Church has convened twenty-one general councils during the twenty centuries of its existence. The twenty-first council is also known as the Second Vatican Council, which met from 1962 to 1965. Within the Roman Catholic tradition these councils have always been times when the bishops of the church could discuss doctrine and practice (faith and life), and find ways to keep the church current with their understanding of God's will. These councils have always been preceded by great conflict over issues of contemporary relevance, and have been called to seek common understandings on those issues.

The positive outcomes of Vatican II include giving the bishops more authority in church affairs (more equality with the pope), allowing the use of the vernacular language (rather than Latin) in church services, elevating the importance of personal Bible reading by the laity, recognizing the importance of religious liberty for all Christians, recognizing the equality of the Orthodox and Catholic churches (i.e., lifting the ban of excommunication against the Eastern church which was imposed in A.D. 1054), and encouraging interaction of Catholics with Orthodox and Protestant churches.

Notes

Chapter 1

1. Hocker and Wilmot, *Interpersonal Conflict*, 4th ed. (Madison, Wis.: Wm. C. Brown, 1995).

2. *Facilitation* allows a third party to sit in on a conversation and help the primary parties talk together in a fair, open, and honest manner. *Conciliation* is described by some as inviting a respected third party to hear both sides separately, and then privately advise each party how the conflict should be resolved. This is an especially important approach in some cultures, and in some cross-cultural conflict transformation.

Conciliation may be a prelude to bringing parties together for direct dialogue, as in facilitation or mediation. Where direct dialogue is culturally impermissible or otherwise impractical, the conciliator facilitates the exchange of communications by shuttling between key parties until a consensus is negotiated or otherwise acceptable closure is reached. As conciliators work within various cultures, they may encourage believers to explore ways of implementing Jesus' teaching on direct dialogue in Matthew 18:15.

3. See *Mennonite Conciliation Service Training Manual*, pp. 15-8, 19-20, 35-6, 61-2, and the Mennonite Conciliation Service video *Conflict in the Church: Division or Diversity?* (see p. 55-57 of this manual for ordering information).

Chapter 2

1. Much of the information in this chapter is based on the work of Speed Leas, *Moving Your Church Through Conflict* (Bethesda, Md.: The Alban Institute, 1985).

2. In history, a holy war has always been defined as a war sanctioned by God, in which his human servants root out evil by destructive forces. The Crusades were viewed as holy wars by the Christian crusaders. Islamic fundamentalists have also viewed the *jihad* (holy war in Arabic) as sanctioned by God to destroy the non-Islamic enemy.

Chapter 3

1. Cross-stitching here refers to a wide variety of individuals in a congregation sharing their views with each other, and not only with their closest friends. Congregations that are open systems have less difficulty with destructive conflict, because they are not threatened by diverse opinions, and know how to work through such differences and "confusion."

2. Feedback is the same in indirect cultures, but it happens differently. For example, if someone has a problem with the time set for a meeting, that information works its way back to the person who started the idea. This avoids potential for loss of face for the organizer, since a time, place, and who should attend is established through the grapevine by consensus. In this way, there is no possibility of the meeting being set when someone who should be there can't come.

3. Everett J. Thomas, ed., *A Mennonite Polity for Ministerial Leadership* (Newton, Kan.: Faith & Life Press, 1996), 113-4.

4. Carolyn Shrock-Shenk, ed., *Mediation and Facilitation Training Manual*, 4th ed. (Akron, Pa.: Mennonite Conciliation Service, 2000).

5. See Marlin Thomas, "Turning Abusive Conflict into Opportunities for Reconciliation," *Gospel Herald* (May 27, 1997), 6-7 for an elaboration of people abuses.

Chapter 4

1. "Characteristics of Good Process," in *Mediation and Facilitation Training Manual*, 4th ed., Carolyn Schrock-Shenk, ed. (Akron, Pa.: Mennonite Conciliation Service, 2000), 211. Chapter 5, "Group Facilitation and Discernment," provides excellent insights into planning and implementing healthy problem-solving strategies.

2. Of the disciples, two were called "Sons of Thunder," one was a Zealot, one was a mystic (he was found praying under a sycamore tree), one (Andrew) was a shy leader, one was a Judean and a thief, one seemingly always got his foot in his mouth, and one was a former tax collector, to name a few.

3. A complete version of the document may be secured at http://peace.Mennolink.org.

About the Authors

Larry Dunn is currently an associate in the Center for Peacemaking and Conflict Studies at Fresno Pacific University. He previously served with Mennonite Central Committee in Labrador (Canada) as a cross-cultural conflict consultant working with aboriginal communities on community justice, self-government, and land rights issues and was six years the executive director for Eastern Pennsylvania Mediation Service. He and his wife and three sons attend College Community Mennonite Brethren Church, Clovis, California.

Duane Ruth-Heffelbower is professor of Conflict Management and Peacemaking at Fresno Pacific University Graduate School, serving in the Center for Peacemaking and Conflict Studies as associate director. He is the author of several books and articles on conflict resolution, including *Conflict and Peacemaking Across Cultures: Training for Trainers*. He and his wife are members of Mennonite Community Church, Fresno, California.

Alice M. Price is a private mediator, trainer, and dispute resolution consultant in southern Colorado. She also directs a Victim-Offender Reconciliation Program part-time. Alice previously served as director of Mennonite Conciliatory Service where she also edited the *Conciliation Quarterly*. She resides in La Jara, Colorado, with her husband and daughter. She is a member of Mennonite Church of La Jara.

Marlin E. Thomas is president of Resources for Resolving Conflict, Inc. and has served the church as a congregational transformation pastor and consultant for over fifteen years. He is the author of numerous articles and books on conflict resolution, including *A Study of Conflict in the Bible* and *Resolving Disputes in Christian Groups*. He lives with his wife in Lancaster, Pennsylvania.

Notes